S0-AFM-606

THE SUCCESSFUL HIGH SCHOOL ATHLETIC PROGRAM

THE SUCCESSFUL HIGH SCHOOL ATHLETIC PROGRAM

by Robert L. Purdy

PARKER PUBLISHING COMPANY, INC. West Nyack, N. Y.

Library of Congress Cataloging in Publication Data

Purdy, Robert L (date)
The successful high school athletic program.

Bibliography: p.
1. Physical education and training--Administration.
I. Title.
GV343.5.P8 375'.6137 72-8458
ISBN 0-13-862847-5

Printed in the United States of America

To my wife, Dorothy

With special thanks to Mr. Rex Smith, Director of Athletics, Parma Public Schools, Parma, Ohio; Dr. Roswell Merrick, Assistant Secretary, American Association of Health, Physical Education and Recreation, and Dr. Harold Meyer, Commissioner, Ohio High School Athletic Association.

Wherefore seeing we also are compassed about with so great a cloud of witnesses, let us lay aside every weight, and the sin which doth so easily beset us, and let us run with patience the race that is set before us. Hebrews 12:1

THE PURPOSE OF THIS BOOK

This book is a practical approach to dealing with the more important facets of administering and directing a successful high school athletic program. Such areas as communication, policies and procedures, financial aspects, police protection and crowd control, insurance program, public relations, game night procedures, and eligibility problems are covered.

The book was written to serve as a guideline in developing a worthwhile and functional athletic program. Problems discussed in this book are of frequent concern to most directors.

Those men who are actively involved in the administration of a high school athletic program will find this book helpful. It can also be worthwhile to those who are relatively inexperienced in such positions and to men who recently were appointed to direct athletic programs.

The real benefit derived from this book is the day-to-day application of practical solutions to major athletic problems. Each athletic director has a similar situation and yet each one has different and varied concerns.

The major areas in athletic administration adaptable to school systems of all sizes will be stressed. The philosophy and organization necessary to conduct a successful program is of paramount importance to all concerned.

Never before has interscholastic athletics been confronted by so many major problems and concerns as today. We are truly at the crossroads. The future lies in the hands of well-trained, dedicated athletic directors.

Chapter by chapter, this book illustrates a unique approach in developing a sound athletic program which will be readily accepted, in application, as a vital part of the school curriculum.

Emphasis is placed on the important role that competent athletic administrators must play in organizing, supervising, and directing their programs.

This book stresses the great need for sound organization in all areas of the program, as well as the need for harmonious relations with the many organizations, associations, and clubs involved and associated with these programs.

Bob Purdy

Contents

The Purpose of This Book . 7

1. **Principles and Organization for Successful Athletic Administration • 15**

   Basic philosophy
   Proper consideration of all sports
   Athletics: A vital part of the curriculum
   Role of the superintendent and the board of education
   Professional responsibility
   Basic principles for program

2. **Developing Effective Policies, Procedures, and Communication Channels for the Athletic Department • 22**

   Committee involved
   Area assignments
   Format for handbook
   Duties and responsibilities of principals, directors of athletics, faculty managers, and coaches.
   Monthly reports to board of education
   Use of handbooks and manuals
   Annual athletic report

3. **Establishing Confident Relations Between Administration and Coaches • 35**

   Cooperation of superintendent and board of education
   Cooperation of personnel director and principals
   Role of the athletic director
   Employment of coaches
   Assignment and supervision of coaches

3. Establishing Confident Relations Between Administration and Coaches (*Cont*)

Implementation of new procedures
Annual evaluation of the program

4. Developing Persuasive Public Relations with Parents and Community • 49

Dealings with press, radio and television
Cooperation with local service clubs
Active participation in boosters clubs
"Special nights" honoring parents
General procedures

5. Financing a Productive Interscholastic Athletic Program on Any Budget • 61

Role of the Boosters Club
Involvement of the Board of Education
Assistance of service clubs
Special money raising projects
Physical Education Department budget
Responsibility of the Athletic Department

6. Building and Sustaining a Harmonious Physical Education and Intramural Program • 77

Development of a senior high school physical education program
Development of a secondary school intramural program
Cooperation between the interscholastic, physical education, and intramural programs
Assignment of personnel

7. Procuring and Maintaining Athletic Equipment and Facilities • 93

Basic principles
Specific guidelines
Bid buying procedures
Cleaning and reconditioning
Facilities construction
Maintenance program
Care and maintenance of artificial turf

8. Developing Relevant Eligibility Procedures for Athletes • 108

Basic responsibility
Procedure in each building
Communication with teachers
Role of the athletic director

8. Developing Relevant Eligibility Procedures for Athletes (*Cont*)

Coaches' cooperation
Status of the ineligible player
Maintaining an amateur status

9. Building Schedules, Hiring Officials, and Dealing with Transportation • 122

Conference affiliation and relations with other schools
Advance planning in scheduling
Assignment of officials
Treatment and cooperation with officials
Responsibility for chartering team buses
Policies and rules for spectator buses

10. Determining and Applying Dependable Game Day Procedures • 137

Basic check list and plans
Gate help assignment
Ushers and program sellers
City police
Meeting with officials
Team physician and trainer
Custodial responsibilities
Role of cheerleaders
Band participation

11. Utilizing Police Protection and Crowd Control Effectively at Athletic Events • 152

A planned procedure
The law and the spectator
Community involvement
The "supportive" people
Responsibilities of state and national associations

12. Designing a Balanced System for Honoring Athletes and for Developing Girls' Interscholastic Athletics . 170

Basic policy for banquets
Basic policy for assemblies
Award system
General programs–Rules coverage and regulations for contests
Involvement of Boosters Clubs and service clubs

13. Implementing Advantageous Insurance and Medical Assistance for the Athletic Program • 190

School insurance plan
State approved activity accident plan
Catastrophic insurance
Policy on handling athletic injuries
Physical examination
The field of sports medicine

14. Developing a Dynamic Cheerleader Program • 203

Clinics for cheerleaders
Cheerleader selection plan
Award system and eligibility
Developing a handbook
School spirit

15. Organizing and Maintaining a Strong Junior High School Athletic Program • 217

Standards for junior high school athletics
Membership in state association
Rules and regulations
Junior high athletic program offered
Association with other schools

16. Professional Growth and Participation in State and National Associations . 231

Professional preparation of athletic directors
Certification of high school coaches
District, state, and national associations
Policies governing attendance at clinics and meetings
Professional behavior of athletic directors
Future trends in school athletics

Index • 257

THE SUCCESSFUL HIGH SCHOOL ATHLETIC PROGRAM

ONE

Principles and Organization for Successful Athletic Administration

One of the most important principles necessary for organizing and conducting a successful program of any nature lies within the framework of its own basic philosophy. This in turn will affect the professional attitude and approach for that particular program. Developing and directing secondary school athletic programs requires such a philosophy.

Many educators have excellent aims and objectives and apply these well to their schools and departments. Many others surprisingly enough lack the guiding principles that a sound philosophy can afford.

BASIC PHILOSOPHY

Countless people go through life without really knowing what kind of vocation or profession to follow. Still others hold down responsible positions but lack the foresight and direction that is so necessary in any work.

We in athletics should ask ourselves just what is our basic philosophy? What do I stand for? What am I really trying to accomplish?

This simple philosophy which I have attempted to follow has been most helpful to me: We must offer the best possible facilities, and conducted by the best available personnel. To achieve this to our complete satisfaction may be impossible; but to work diligently towards this goal should mean a successful program.

PROPER CONSIDERATION OF ALL SPORTS

The old theory of major and minor sports is rapidly dwindling away. All sports are important and should receive proper consideration. Budgets will vary and attendance at certain types of games varies considerably from others. But the fact remains that young athletes are getting an opportunity to compete in a worthwhile activity, which otherwise may not have been possible.

Dr. Paul Briggs, Superintendant of the Cleveland City Schools, is a strong advocate of large athletic programs involving as many students as possible. The value of athletics in the inner city becomes increasingly important. The "task force," which was formed to study crowd control problems at athletic events in Cleveland, was in complete accord.

ATHLETICS: A VITAL PART OF THE CURRICULUM

One of the many obstacles that have confronted people in interscholastic athletics has been the great misnomer that their program is an entity unto itself, that it is not actually a part of the curriculum. It has good qualities but must be self-supporting so that other departments are not deprived of allocated monies in the budget. The coaches are not really interested in teaching, but are only concerned about the success of their athletic teams. And so it goes.

Part of this stigma has been the result of slipshod programs conducted by people who were not really interested in education per se. We are also guilty at times of trying to fight our way through problems, rather than trying to be a part of the team that helps build a better curriculum.

There are encouraging signs that point to a breakthrough regarding this situation. The passage of state legislation which enables boards of education to use public tax monies for financing approved co-curricular activities is proving most helpful.

A national movement is underway to help develop joint projects between the athletic department and the art department. Pilot projects are going in Rosslyn, Long Island; Parma, Ohio; Princeton, New Jersey; and the New York City Public Schools. The art departments are having children of all grade levels express sports experiences through art media such as painting, clay, wire, etc. The outstanding art pieces are displayed at an exhibit.

Informal receptions for the artists, their families, and faculty, sponsored by the art department and athletic department, may follow the exhibits.

The National Council of Secondary School Athletic Directors has been instrumental in promoting this project.

Different athletic conferences are expanding their programs to include competition in debate, chorus, intramural activities, band concerts, and one act plays. Students, teachers, and administrators welcome this opportunity to associate with member schools in activities other than athletics.

The athletic program which is centered around the welfare of the students will become a vital part of the curriculum.

ROLE OF THE SUPERINTENDENT AND BOARD OF EDUCATION

The superintendent of schools and the board of education will administer the athletic program in much the same manner as the other programs. Their philosophy toward conducting a sound program will help to determine the course that is followed. It will also lend support to the principal, director of athletics, and coaches when pressured from certain community groups.

More specifically their philosophy should include the following areas:

First, to encourage a state required program for professional preparation of coaches.

Second, to employ good coaches who are also very capable classroom teachers.

Third, to conduct a program with maximum participation for both boys and girls.

Fourth, to provide the best facilities possible and to properly maintain these facilities.

Fifth, to encourage a good communication system to the athletic staff through the director and in return to the board of education and the superintendent of schools.

Sixth, to consider the athletic program as an integral part of the curriculum.

There are other areas that could be included but the ones already mentioned are most significant.

PROFESSIONAL RESPONSIBILITY

The role that athletic director must play has never been more important. The many challenges confronting our people and programs today are staggering. The constant need to improve and upgrade the program requires the guidance and direction of a real professional. We as athletic directors must fill this role.

The February 1970 issue of the *Athletic Director* published by the National Council of Secondary school Athletic Directors gives an excellent insight as to what a profession actually is:

A profession is not a collection of individuals who get a living for themselves by the same kind of work, or who organize and act to protect themselves as a separate entity from the normal forces of society.

A profession is a functioning group of specially qualified persons whose common endeavors are basic in the stream of social development. A profession is an association of persons certified by a recognized authority for social purposes, responsibilities, and goals. The essence of a profession is in its group action as the members assume self-realized responsibilities to society under a recognized administrative framework of the group. It is organized so that:

1. Within the group its members can help one another in the development of their own professional competence as together they face mutual problems in their field.
2. The group can express that which the majority of its members believe relative to any item of professional significance which may arise. Example: By a consensus of opinion expressed through the channels of their organization, they may make a stand against the practices of others, by a censure of certain kinds of conduct on the grounds that a practice, though satisfying to the individual or other members, is adjudged to weaken efforts of all other members, the group effort. Such censure calls upon faith in group opinions, group spirit, and group purpose.
3. Group relationships can be formed to speed achievement of the goals of the organization by the group helping and giving strength to its individual members.

The same publication (the February, 1970 issue of the *Athletic Director*) has a check list for athletic directors to determine if they are true professionals. The eight criteria are listed below:

1. Members of professions solicit and accept only the best qualified men to their professional ranks.
2. Persons applying for admission must undergo an extended period of training to meet established requirements of the profession. During these preparatory years, they acquire a broad cultural education, a thorough understanding of the principles upon which the profession is based, and a mastery of the competencies their work requires.
3. To protect the public against incompetent practitioners, professional men secure a state license to practice or some other form of control which regulates their admission to membership.
4. Members of professions keep studying and broadening the fields of knowledge of their profession.
5. Members of professions are usually motivated by a desire to serve mankind coupled with intense interest in the profession.
6. To promote their interests and improve ethical standards, they usually join with some organization of their respective profession.
7. Professional men make their chosen work a lifetime career. After entering a specific field, they serve their fellow men until they retire from practice.
8. Members of professions establish codes of ethics. These codes are not state laws but rather group-imposed standards of approved behavior for all members to observe in their relationships with associates and the public.

BASIC PRINCIPLES FOR ATHLETIC PROGRAM

The philosophy of a sound athletic program must be firmly engrained in basic principles and applied to the particular program.

The Division of Men's Athletics of the American Association for Health, Physical Education, and Recreation (a department of the National Education Association) published a platform statement entitled "Athletics in Education." This was printed in 1963 but still applies today.

A portion of this statement follows:

INTERSCHOLASTIC AND INTERCOLLEGIATE ATHLETIC PROGRAMS

To utilize fully the potential in athletics for educational experiences, interscholastic and intercollegiate athletic programs should be organized and conducted in accordance with these six basic principles.

1. Interscholastic and intercollegiate athletic programs should be regarded as integral parts of the total educational program and should be so conducted that they are worthy of such regard.

2. Interscholastic and intercollegiate athletic programs should supplement rather than serve as substitutes for basic physical education programs, physical recreation programs, and intramural athletic programs.

3. Interscholastic and intercollegiate athletic programs should be subject to the same administrative control as the total education program.

4. Interscholastic and intercollegiate athletic programs should be conducted by men with adequate training in physical education.

5. Interscholastic and intercollegiate athletic programs should be so conducted that the physical welfare and safety of the participants is protected and fostered.

6. Interscholastic and intercollegiate athletic programs should be conducted in accordance with the letter and the spirit of the rules and regulations of appropriate conference, state, and national athletic associations.

In Elementary Schools: Athletics between schools should be limited to informal games between teams from two or more schools and to occasional sports days when teams from several schools assemble for a day of friendly, informal competition. At such events, emphasis should be placed on participation by all students. The attendance of spectators (particularly students as spectators) should be discouraged. High-pressure programs of interscholastic athletics, in which varsity teams compete in regularly scheduled contests that are attended by partisan spectators, should not be allowed under any circumstances.

In Junior High Schools: Limited programs of interscholastic athletics that are adapted to the capacities and the needs of junior high school boys are desirable. The physical and emotional immaturity of the junior high youngster requires that such programs be controlled with extreme care to ensure that primary emphasis is placed on providing educational experiences for the participants rather than on producing winning teams, and that the physical welfare of the participants is protected.

In Senior High Schools: Interscholastic athletic programs should include team and dual sports of a variety compatible with the enrollment, the equipment and facilities, and the professional personnel in the school. Every effort should be extended to provide opportunities for all interested boys to participate.

In Colleges and Universities: Intercollegiate athletic programs should include as many team, dual, and individual sports as finances will permit. Such programs should be conducted in strict adherence to the rules and regulations of the appropriate governing body.

PROFESSIONAL PERSONNEL

Athletics at every level should be conducted by professionally prepared personnel of unquestionable integrity who are dedicated to the task of developing their charges to the highest degree possible—mentally, physically, and morally.

In addition to a knowledge of athletics, such personnel should have a knowledge of (1) the place and purpose of athletics in education, (2) the growth and development of children and youth, (3) the effects of exercise on the human organism, and (4) first aid. Certain basic competencies in physical education, specifically applicable to the welfare and success of participants in competitive sports, should be a minimum prerequisite for teaching or coaching athletics at any level.

TWO

Developing Effective Policies, Procedures, and Communication Channels for the Athletic Department

No athletic program can efficiently operate without being sound in its basic organization. An effective and functional handbook of policies and procedures is of paramount importance in establishing the necessary groundwork.

The purpose of this chapter is to help establish guidelines for developing practical and useful handbooks and other communication channels.

COMMITTEE INVOLVED IN DEVELOPING POLICIES AND PROCEDURES

In order to develop a policies and procedures handbook that is not only operative but acceptable, the athletic director must involve a number of key people. This group should include all head coaches, selected assistant coaches, secondary school principals, the director of athletics, faculty managers, cheerleader coaches, and the superintendent of schools or his assistant.

It will be necessary to call several meetings with a limited number of areas being discussed at each session. Before moving on to the next item in the handbook, there must be a general agreement as to the operational procedure for each topic that is being considered.

The different areas that are to be included may vary somewhat with the school system and the specific needs they are trying to meet.

AREA ASSIGNMENTS

The following areas were developed by the athletic committee of the Berea City Schools and compiled into a practical and workable book.

Table of Contents

Introduction

1. Announcements
2 Annual Reports (interscholastic, intramural, and cheerleader reports)
3. Athletic Assemblies
4. Athletic Council
5. Attendance–Day of Contest
6. Awards
7. Banquets
8. Bills and Payment
9. Building Permits
10. Budgets
11. Changing Sports in Mid-season
12. Coaching Assignments
13. Concessions
14. Contracts for Games and Officials
15. Doctors and Medical Attention
16. Eligibility
17. Ending Date for Season
18. Equipment
19. Facilities
20. Gate Help
21. Injuries
22. Insurance Program

23. Interschool Practice Sessions
24. Money Raising Projects
25. Monthly Board Reports
26. Officials
27. Ohio High School Athletic Association Rules and Regulations
28. Physical Examinations
29. Police Protection
30. Programs
31. Publicity
32. Purchasing
33. Reservations on Trips
34. Scheduling
35. Scouting
36. Scrimmage Games
37. State Meet Chaperones
38. Ticket Procedures
39. Transportation
40. Vocational Education Courses–Eligibility

In order to better illustrate these policies and procedures a few specific items will be discussed.

AREA #3–ASSEMBLIES

1. Arrangements for regular athletic awards assemblies will be made by the director of athletics through the principals at the high schools. The faculty managers will make the necessary arrangements through the principals at the junior high level.
2. Approval of awards by the athletic councils must be received at least one week before the assembly.
3. All of the school's award assemblies will be held as soon as possible after the final contest of that particular season.
4. Occasionally other athletic assemblies in the form of films, rules interpretations, demonstrations, etc. may be presented.
5. Pep assemblies should be arranged by the cheerleader coaches through the principals at both senior and junior high school levels. These should be short and well organized. They should precede key games on the schedule. A limited number for each sport is encouraged.

AREA #15–DOCTORS AND MEDICAL ATTENTION

1. A doctor shall be in attendance at all high school and junior high school football games both home and away. No school should be scheduled where they are not willing to arrange for a doctor to be present. The director of athletics is responsible for furnishing doctors at all home football games.
2. An attempt will be made to have the team physician in attendance at away high school football games.
3. The director of athletics will arrange for a doctor to be present at such events as the sectional and district wrestling tournaments, the Berea Relays, district swimming meets, conference track meets, etc.
4. A trainer will be in attendance at all high school football practice sessions and games (varsity, reserve, and junior varsity).
5. All serious or questionable injuries should be referred to the team physician. The physician shall make the decision as to when the boy is ready to play or practice.

AREA #16–ELIGIBILITY

1. Regular standards of eligibility will be governed by the rules and regulations of the Ohio High School Athletic Association.
2. Eligibility regulations other than those established by the Ohio High School Athletic Association shall be determined by the athletic council and the building principal.
3. Problems of intra-school eligibility shall be decided by the building principal.
4. In all cases the building principal is responsible for eligibility matters.
5. It is recommended that eligibility lists be put in the teacher's mail boxes for a weekly check on the athletes they have in class.
6. At least once each semester, an explanation concerning general principles of eligibility should be discussed at a regular faculty meeting.
7. The director of athletics should make available to the teachers any necessary information regarding eligibility questions.

Format for the Handbook

The format for this handbook should consist of the following items.

1. A table of contents.
2. Introduction—This should be prepared and written by the superintendent of schools or director of athletics.
3. Purpose of the handbook—This should include an explanation as to how this manual was devised, who was involved in its preparation, etc.
4. Various areas included and the policies and procedures pertaining to each.
5. Summary—This should include such things as periodic revisions and supplements issued covering new or altered policies between actual revisions of the entire handbook.

DUTIES AND RESPONSIBILITIES OF KEY ATHLETIC PERSONNEL

In addition to the policies and procedures handbook, it is advisable to have duties and responsibilities spelled out for key athletic personnel. Such positions as the building principal, director of athletics, faculty manager of athletics, head coach, assistant coach, and the cheerleader advisor should be included.

These general personnel policies serve as excellent guidelines for new and experienced people in the athletic program. They can also be helpful in school systems where state laws require that school personnel receiving additional pay for coaching or similar duties must sign a supplementary pay contract. These duties and responsibilities may also be compiled in a handbook. In turn the supplementary pay contracts may refer to the handbook rather than list these duties separately for each person affected.

These duties and responsibilities may vary in different schools, especially in such positions as the director of athletics and the faculty manager of athletics. There is also the possibility that both of these positions are handled by one man. In some cases there will be an athletic director for the system and faculty manager of athletics in each building.

Specific job descriptions follow:

Secondary School Principals:

1. The administrative head of the school shall be held ultimately responsible in all matters pertaining to interscholastic athletic activities involving his school (OHSAA Constitution and Rules, 1963-64, Rule 4, Section 1.)
2. The Principal shall fulfill all duties and responsibilities as they pertain to interscholastic athletics as prescribed by the State High School Athletic Association.
3. He shall serve as a member of the junior or senior high school Athletic Council.

Director of Athletics

1. Function of Job:
   The director of athletics reports to the assistant superintendent of schools in charge of instruction. All coaches, faculty managers, cheerleader sponsors, and intramural directors report to the director of athletics.
   The primary responsibility of the director of athletics is to supervise the interscholastic athletic program, the intramural program and the cheerleader program at the secondary schools. This position involves approximately 10½ to 11 months work including vacations during the school year and practically every weekend, including Saturday nights. Many meetings are held after school and after supper during the week, which demand additional time.
2. Specific Duties:
   a. Prepare annual reports, intramural handbooks, policies and procedures booklets.
   b. Work with the principal and faculty manager on all athletic assemblies.
   c. Prepare agenda and serve as a member of athletic councils at both high schools.
   d. Supervise awards system for the program.
   e. Make arrangements for athletic banquets at the high schools, work closely with service clubs in the area.
   f. Responsibility for building permits involving athletics at all secondary schools for games at home and away.
   g. Interview new applicants and help assign all coaches in our system.

h. Arrange for concessions for all athletic events at stadium.
i. Hire officials for all athletic events and do scheduling for all schools.
j. Arrange for doctors at all home football games and larger athletic events such as sectional wrestling meets.
k. Work closely with principals, guidance counselors, and the state high school athletic association on eligibility problems.
l. Supervise and authorize purchase of athletic equipment.
m. Work closely with maintenance people and assistant superintendents regarding facilities.
n. Supervise the insurance program in athletics.
o. Assist in money-raising projects for the schools.
p. Prepare monthly board reports to keep Board of Education and all interested personnel advised as to school athletic projects.
q. Work closely with state high school athletic association in all matters pertaining to rules and regulations of the association.
r. Assist school nurses in setting up physical examinations.
s. Arrange for police protection at all home night athletic events.
t. Work closely with the Boosters Clubs at high schools in preparing the football and basketball programs.
u. Arrange for publicity releases to local newspapers.
v. Handle reservations for any overnight trips such as at state meets in different sports.
w. Make scouting arrangements for football and basketball personnel.
x. Work closely with faculty managers on ticket procedures. Organize pre-season football ticket drives where entire school district is canvassed in tickets sales.
y. Work closely with the principals, superintendent, and assistant superintendents in supervising and coordinating the overall program.
z. Arrange for all team buses through the transportation supervisor.

Senior High School Faculty Manager of Athletics

1. He is responsible for reporting of local games results to the area newspapers.
2. He will arrange for all athletic awards assemblies including the preparation of letters, certificates, etc.
3. He will assist the director of athletics in banquet preparations.
4. He is responsible for the gate help at all home athletic events where admission is charged. He also arranges for ushers, program sellers, student assistants, check room facilities, etc.
5. He handles all ticket sales at his school.
6. He pays the athletic bills, keeps the books, and makes the annual financial statement.
7. He assists the director of athletics in preparing the budgets.
8. He is responsible for student spectator buses.
9. All athletic announcements in his building are cleared through him.
10. He is responsible for the organization and sale of student activities cards.

Duties and Responsibilities of the Head Coach

The head coach is the person most instrumental in crowd control. His behavior on the field or athletic contest area will greatly influence the reaction of the spectators as well as team members. His behavior and conduct must be of the highest caliber. He shall:

1. Be responsible for all matters pertaining to the organization and administration of the coaching of the team under his direction and shall enforce all rules of the Ohio High School Athletic Association as they pertain to the respective sports.
2. Assign duties to all assistant coaches and evaluate the performance of these assistant coaches as they fulfill their duties and responsibilities.
3. Plan and conduct all practice sessions. (The suggested length of an actual practice is 90 minutes.)

4. Be responsible for preparing public information releases regarding their particular sport. Telephone or personal interviews, when requested by news agencies, are not here considered as press releases. In requested interviews, coaches and others connected with the athletic program should bear in mind that their statements are published and read by people who are for and against the school's program. Consequently, these statements should be carefully weighed and considered before they are given to the news media personnel.
5. Maintain an accurate squad roster at all times, being sure that it is up-to-date and on file with the faculty manager and principal. Roster to bear coaches' signatures and date.
6. Cooperate with the athletic director in establishing physical examination schedules and verify that no candidate is issued equipment or allowed to practice until he has completed his physical exam card. Card is signed by parents and any insurance coverage to be taken is in force.
7. Assign at least one coach to be with the squad at all times. This includes locker room supervision until all squad members have left the building and then seeing that all windows and exit doors are locked in any area that has been used by their athletic team during the course of that particular practice session.
8. Prepare a detailed equipment and supply budget request to be submitted to the Director of Athletics no later than the first week in February.
9. Inspect all equipment, oversee the issuance and collection of equipment, maintain equipment inventory records, and direct activities of student managers; also, enforce rules regarding care of equipment. Advise the Director of Athletics as to reconditioning of equipment needs.
10. Conduct all staff meetings and be in charge of all tryouts, practices, team meetings and athletic contests insofar as the team is involved.
11. Arrange for presentation of team awards through the faculty manager and principal. Provide the faculty manager with roster of recommended award winners.

12. Recommend to the Athletic Director teams that may be scheduled and officials to be employed.
13. Serve as an advisor to the students on his squad and to help them, by advice or direction, with problems.
14. Instruct team members that equipment is to be worn only for the purpose for which it was purchased, namely, for practice sessions and game competition for interscholastic athletics. It is not to be worn at any social event, or throughout the community other than at athletic sessions.
15. Announce and enforce rules and regulations pertaining to conditioning of players and training rules affecting the health and safety of the players.
16. Report injuries of participants to the proper school officials, including principal and athletic director. Coaches are cautioned to exercise great care in dealing with all injuries and particularly those that are of a serious nature and arouse public interest. In all cases, the coach should assure himself personally that the injured boy is receiving competent medical care and that full reports have been made relative to the injury. Following injuries of a serious or prolonged nature, the coach should secure the signed approval of the doctor and parents before the boy is allowed to again participate in athletic activities.
17. Be interested and loyal to the school's program. He is expected to support the entire program and to be an active participant in striving to improve the athletic program as well as the total educational program of the schools.
18. Be expected, after decisions and policies have been established, to support and conform to them, both in fact and in spirit.
19. Acknowledge that he is the recognized leader and director of his particular sport. He may make decisions of a general nature that are in keeping with the established policies and procedures of the school. However, when decisions affect other coaches and other sports, or when the problem is one that clearly falls within the jurisdiction of the Athletic Council, decision should be delayed

until the Council has discussed the matter fully and reached a decision.

Duties and Responsibilities of Assistant Coach

1. Support the head coach in conducting of the athletic program of that particular sport and the total athletic program of the Berea City School System in general.
2. Be loyal to the coach and to the team. He may have to give up some of his own thoughts regarding team strategy, etc., to fit into the overall pattern as set forth by the head coach.
3. Attend staff meetings when called by the head coach.
4. Assist with scouting of varsity games in football and basketball (this is also true for junior high coaches.)
5. Assume any duties assigned him by the head coach pertaining to the overall athletic program of the particular sport. Some of these duties might be:

   Conducting of portions of practice drills, handling equipment, determining eligibility, working with student managers, scouting, public relations, statistics, etc.

6. In the absence of the head coach, he shall assume all responsibilities herein designated as those of the head coach.

Duties and Responsibilities of Cheerleader Sponsor

1. Be the one person making the final decision as to selection of members of the cheerleading squad.
2. Supervise and conduct tryouts and practices in accord with prescribed directions.
3. Accompany cheerleader squads to and from athletic contests as well as during the contest itself. (A faculty member appointed by the principal may substitute for cheerleader sponsor.)
4. Maintain an inventory of all equipment and supplies.
5. Submit a detailed budget request along with inventory to the Director of Athletics no later than Friday of first week of February.
6. Provide the faculty manager with a list of award winners and type of awards to be ordered.

MONTHLY REPORTS TO THE BOARD OF EDUCATION

One of the best possible media for communication is a monthly report to the board of education. Too often in athletics we assume that people are aware of the many events and activities that are taking place. Many times we are mistaken.

It is the responsibility of the director of athletics to constantly inform the board of education, administration, coaching staffs, intramural directors, etc. of current trends and other important data.

Items included in this report may be the agenda for conference business meetings, banquet preparations, forthcoming assemblies, important athletic dates, special occasions such as clinics, invitational meets, etc. It is most important to also include the intramural activities of the secondary schools in this report.

This serves as a good news release in many instances and keeps the staff members better informed of the many activities in the program in all of the schools.

USE OF HANDBOOKS AND MANUALS

Handbooks, and manuals are only as good as the use to which they are put. All new athletic personnel should be given this information and should be required to read it.

It is often times advisable to have meetings to help clarify certain policies and procedures and on occasion to change or modify some areas. The issuing of periodic memoranda may help to emphasize the importance of different policies.

Head coaches must be well aware of their responsibilities and constantly supervise their assistants as they carry out their duties.

The successful operation of any athletic program depends largely on the cooperation and loyalty of all people involved. Each coach must be willing to abide by the rules as they pertain to all athletic events and not try to go his own way.

Separate handbooks are used in the intramural program and in the cheerleading program as well. These will be referred to in Chapters 6 and 14.

ANNUAL ATHLETIC REPORT

The preparation of an annual athletic report is no easy task. At the same time it can be one of the best projects that you undertake.

The report should be divided into three sections, namely fall, winter, and spring. It includes write-ups by the head coaches, cheerleader coaches, intramural directors, junior varsity coaches, and junior high school coaches. The report is compiled by the director of athletics.

The format for the interscholastic report is as follows:

1. Names of squad members—indicate letter winners, captains, managers, etc.
2. Schedule played and results of games, meets, or matches.
3. Indicate new records set for the season as to individual performance, team scoring, etc.
4. List any special honors received by team members.
5. A brief summary of the season and suggestions for improving your program.

Deadline dates for the interscholastic report should be established. Fall reports are due on December 1; winter reports are due on April 1; and spring reports are due on June 1.

The format for the intramural and cheerleaders reports is as follows:

1. Number of participants in the program.
2. Number and types of events in which they participated.
3. Special group or individual honors and awards.
4. Short statement concerning the program and activities.
5. Plans for next year's program and suggestions for improvement.

The deadline for these reports would be June 1.

The report is distributed to the board of education members, the administration, and all other people involved in the program. It is especially valuable information for new principals, new coaches, and for newspaper reporters. It also serves as an excellent reference source for many different items.

THREE

Establishing Confident Relations Between the Administration and Coaches

Much has been said and written about good rapport between employees of the board of education and lay people in the community. A somewhat newer trend reflects the relationship between the different administrators, the director of athletics and the members of the coaching staff.

This chapter deals with the increased importance of the cooperation of all people involved in the athletic program. It stresses the significance of properly assigning and supervising the coaching staff. It also includes an evaluation of the personnel and the program itself.

COOPERATION OF THE SUPERINTENDENT AND THE BOARD OF EDUCATION

The ultimate success of any program requires the cooperation, understanding and leadership which must be provided by the superintendent of schools and board of education.

Oftentimes questions are asked such as: How do the superintendent and board of education relate to the athletic program? Are they advised of present achievements and pending problems? Are they made aware of new procedures which could materially affect the present program? Do we work closely with them in evaluating our program and in making the necessary improvements?

The superintendent of schools should be interested in all activities. He must be aware of their importance and work to maintain a proper relationship of these activities to the total educational program. A proper balance of many activities will provide a better and more complete educational program.

As directors of athletics and coaches we must be willing to cooperate with the superintendent in order to implement such a program. We cannot expect his cooperation and support if we are unwilling to meet our responsibilities as they pertain to the total school picture.

We must involve the superintendent as a guest, as a participant, and as a spectator.

The role of the board of education is most significant. They make the policies for the school system and the superintendent is charged with properly administering these policies. As directors of athletics we should be certain that the more important aspects of our program are included in the board of education policies. These recommendations pertaining to athletics should receive the principal's approval before sending them to the superintendent.

We must encourage the board of education to take an active part in our program. They too can get involved as guests, participants, and spectators.

Many times we are guilty of poor communication. This in itself can cause problems and misunderstandings. In Chapter Two reference is made to monthly athletic reports to the superintendent of schools and board of education members. This is just one of many ways to keep these people properly informed.

The director of athletics should welcome opportunities to make presentations at the board of education meetings. In most cases it is not advisable for him to attend all such meetings unless supervisors of other areas with comparable positions are also attending.

Coaches, cheerleader advisors, intramural directors, and other members of the athletic department staff should work directly with the director of athletics. They should not go directly to the superintendent with any problem. A failure to follow this policy may cause serious repercussions and could result in much disunity and disorganization.

COOPERATION OF PERSONNEL DIRECTOR AND PRINCIPALS

The director of athletics and the personnel director or a staff member with similar responsibilities need to work closely in developing and maintaining a capable athletic staff. There must be excellent communication and harmony between the men filling these positions.

Although employment of coaches is discussed later in this chapter, this represents one of the main areas requiring good cooperation. In-service training programs for staff members may be cooperatively developed.

Attendance at clinics and professional meetings, promotions to other positions within the system, and recommendations for positions in other systems are common situations requiring joint approval.

Good relationship between the principal and director of athletics is paramount if the athletic program is to be successful. This may vary depending upon the duties and responsibilities of the director of athletics. If he teaches and works all day in one building his relationship will be different from a director for the entire school system.

In either case the director of athletics position is becoming more significant than in the past. He assumes more and more of the athletic responsibilities and corresponding problems each year. Directors lacking professional training and experience may find themselves somewhat restricted in their positions.

Principals are normally charged with the responsibility for conducting the athletic program in their particular building. Since their duties are becoming greater, many of these assignments are being given to the director. He in turn must keep the principal well informed on all areas of the program.

The following aspects of the program are often evaluated by the principal.

1. The amount of participation in each sport and the size of the squads.
2. Rapport between the coaches and parents and between the coaches and other staff members.

3. Financial status of the program including the budget, gate receipts, and general business procedures.
4. Accurate reporting of eligibility lists.
5. Safety aspects and general health and welfare of the athletes.
6. General procedures in conducting a home interscholastic event.
7. Crowd control measures properly administered.
8. Professional growth of the director of athletics and the coaching staff.

ROLE OF THE DIRECTOR OF ATHLETICS

The director of athletics is often times referred to as the "middle man" in establishing good rapport and relations in athletic administration. To be really successful and efficient he must be highly organized and very versatile. He is the key man with widely diversified responsibilities.

Different rating sheets and evaluation prodecures may be used to determine the effectiveness of the athletic program and the director of athletics. The following check list was prepared by Mr. James Perkins, Director of Athletics, Riverside-Brookfield Township High School, Riverside, Illinois. Mr. Perkins was the first President of the National Council of Secondary School Athletic Directors. It gives a very comprehensive coverage of the director's responsibilities for directing and supervising the program.

1. Is the interest of the individual student challenged?
2. Is the program attractive to a fairly large percentage of the student body?
3. Do the athletic director and his staff provide counseling and guidance service for the students?
4. What is the athletic director's role in selecting his staff?
5. What attempt does he make to supervise them in their coaching assignments?
6. Does he encourage individual improvement within the staff by providing books, periodicals, and opportunities to attend clinics and coaching schools?
7. Are the coaches encouraged to continue their graduate study?
8. Is a competitive salary maintained and periodically reviewed?

9. Do the director and his staff belong to and take an active part in the work of their state and national professional organizations?
10. Does the athletic director stay within his budget?
11. Is he knowledgeable in his purchasing and care of equipment?
12. Is careful consideration given to the maintenance and improvement of both the outdoor and indoor facilities?
13. Is the athletic program safety-oriented?
14. Is the athletic director familiar with treatment of injuries and the handling of emergencies and insurance claims?
15. Does the school district abide by all the rules of the state athletic association?
16. Is school liability considered?
17. Does the athletic director possess knowledge of the rules and coaching techniques used in different sports?
18. How effectively are home contests organized and supervised?
19. Does the school have a parent club?
20. How effective is this organization?
21. Does the community call upon the athletic director to act as a consultant or a resource person in helping groups with some of their internal problems and projects?
22. Does he as department head handle clerical work satisfactorily?
23. Is the administration kept up to date on the athletic department business?
24. Are provisions made for press releases, school announcements, and assemblies according to school policy?
25. How well does the athletic director cooperate with the building principal in working toward the realization of the overall goals of the high school?

One area that needs constant attention is the cooperation with the custodial and maintenance staff. Without their assistance no athletic program can possibly exist. Yet how often we are critical of these people or merely take them for granted.

It is true that they are on the payroll, the same as the athletic staff members. However, they merit our appreciation, cooperation, and support for their important contribution.

If at all possible the director of athletics should work directly with the maintenance supervisor on all of these matters. This can help eliminate problems that may result from too many people getting involved in making decisions pertaining to the athletic facilities.

The director of athletics must constantly guard against getting so "mired down" with the detail part of his position. He needs to frequently analyze the effectiveness of his program as it relates to the needs of the staff, the student body, and the community.

EMPLOYMENT OF COACHES

The employment of coaches requires a set policy that must be followed and adhered to by all school systems. It may vary somewhat with different communities and schools, but should be carefully followed in all sports.

Several questions present themselves in considering this undertaking–what are we really looking for? Who should interview the candidates? Who makes the final decision?

Probably the best place to start is with the candidate's credentials as a teacher. Since this is his primary job, and since this work requires most of his time, and since the major part of his salary is based on his teaching position, he must be, first of all, a good teacher. This also adds to his stature with the rest of the staff and with the administration. Any good coach should be a good teacher.

The director of athletics should be involved in the interviews, regardless of the size of the school, as well as the building principal and the personnel director. If an assistant coach is being considered, the head coach should also take part. The superintendent of schools will probably want to interview head coaching candidates in some sports unless the school system is very large.

The final decision naturally rests with the board of education. However, the recommendation of the principal and athletic director are usually approved.

It is always difficult to employ the man we want, who can teach what we want, and who can coach what we want. We must also guard against hiring too many coaches from the same colleges. "In-breeding" may cause cliques and also result in a limitation of new ideas and procedures.

The director of athletics can facilitate the work of filling staff vacancies by communicating closely with the personnel director and principal regarding teaching positions that are still open. The director of athletics should be allotted a certain amount of time to bring in interested candidates for interviews before these positions are filled by non-coaching teachers.

What do the principals, superintendents, and athletic directors expect of a coach? Surprisingly enough, their qualification sheets would be very similar. We should actually expect and insist on several criteria.

1. A competent, cooperative teacher.
2. A man who is genuinely interested in the welfare and safety of the students.
3. One who is interested in professional growth and in implementing new procedures.
4. A coach who is loyal to the administration, to the staff, and to the school.
5. A man who is public relations conscious.
6. One who participates in church and community projects.
7. A person who is willing to do an honest day's work.

The "complete" coach is a rare commodity. The "complete" man in any profession is difficult to find. We must endeavor to employ the best people that we possibly can. We must work diligently with the coaches and all of the staff members through in-service programs designed to improve their capabilities.

ASSIGNMENT AND SUPERVISION OF COACHES

One problem area that seems difficult to overcome is that of assigning coaches to teach in a building where they do not coach. The lack of contact with the students during the normal school day and with the principal of the building where he coaches is not a good situation.

The director of athletics normally does a good job of supervising his coaches during game situations. But far too often he is too busy with the many details involved in his position to attend practice sessions and to observe the staff when no crowd is present. Ask yourself these questions concerning this area:

1) Is the staff really organized?
2) Are the players well disciplined?
3) Is it a real learning situation?

4) Do the drills actually apply to game-like situations?
5) Is there compatibility with all of the staff members?
6) Are the coaches safety concious and prepared to handle injuries?
7) Are the coaches the last ones off the field and the last ones to leave the locker room? Is the locker room properly supervised?
8) Is there proper equipment care?
9) What is the attitude of the players toward the game and toward the coaches?
10) What is the attitude of the coaches toward the players?

This short list of questions can give the director of athletics some worthwhile answers in supervising practice sessions.

Generally speaking, no one should be permitted to coach any team unless he is an employee of the board of education and is a paid member of the coaching staff. There are a few isolated exceptions.

First, there may be well qualified teachers in the school system who are not paid for coaching, but who are capable and interested in assisting with the program. These men should be given limited duties and should be carefully supervised. They may eventually be considered for regular coaching positions.

Second, student teachers who have an adequate background may assist on a limited basis under close supervision.

Third, former athletes who are currently playing on a college team, may give limited assistance during a vacation or prior to the start of the season.

Individual conferences with staff members are a "must." There should include positive and constructive suggestions as well as stressing problem areas and other bad situations. Helpful solutions to these problems should be offered by the director of athletics.

General staff meetings should be held periodically. At these sessions there may be a review of certain policies and procedures, a discussion of problems pertaining to one or all sports, and other items such as the budget, eligibility, assemblies, banquets, etc.

IMPLEMENTATION OF NEW PROCEDURES

The topic of implementation of new procedures requires consid-

Memo

FROM THE DESK OF

JIM WILLIAMS

Athletic Director

erable attention and frequent review. Limitations of facilities, equipment, financial means, and capable personnel can contribute to failure in implementing desirable programs. Advance planning and study with emphasis on need and interest is most desirable.

It is the duty of the director of athletics to inform the administration and his staff of new trends, concepts, and procedures that may improve the present program. Attendance of the director of athletics and other staff members at clinics, workshops, and conventions is imperative. Each school system should have a policy concerning these professional meetings and should have money budgeted for this purpose. The policy should include local, district, state, and national meetings.

The athletic council can serve as an excellent source for initiating plans for new policies and procedures.

ANNUAL EVALUATION OF THE PROGRAM

Few school systems actually take the time to really evaluate their athletic programs. This should be done annually. A committee composed of the superintendent of schools, a board of education member, a secondary school principal, the director of athletics, two head coaches, and two students (a boy and a girl) make a very representative group. They should study such questions as:

First, what are we doing now? Are these areas well received? Is the interest high, is the participation good, and is the organization sound?

Second, in what areas are we most successful? Why is this the case? What is the problem in the other areas? How can we improve these shortcomings?

Third, how did the new phases of our program develop? Should we make any significant changes at this time? If so, what are they?

Fourth, what plans do we have for additional sports? Should we expand our staff to better serve our present program?

Fifth, are there areas that should be deleted? What effect would this have on the program?

Sixth, is our intramural program meeting the needs of the student body? How can it be improved?

The results of this study and appropriate recommendations should be made available to the board of education, the administration, and the members of the athletic staff. Much good can result from such a procedure.

The supervision of members of the athletic staff should include their role in the classroom as well as in a coaching capacity.

The evaluation sheet shown in Figure 3-2 is used by the Parma Public Schools in Parma, Ohio, and was devised by Mr. Rex. B. Smith, director of athletics, physical education, and recreation of this system. The first sheet (Figure 3-1) is used for instruction in filling out the observation form for classroom teachers. A similar form could be used for regular subject matter teachers.

PARMA PUBLIC SCHOOLS
Parma, Ohio

TO: All Health and Physical Education Teachers

FROM: Rex B. Smith, Director of Athletics, Physical Education and Recreation

SUBJECT: Observation Form

This attached form has been prepared as a vehicle to aid in upgrading performance in the teaching of health and physical education.

The procedure for its use will be as follows:

1. You fill out one copy (white)
2. Department Chairman of Physical Education for your building fills out one copy (pink)
3. Director of Athletics, Physical Education and Recreation fills out one copy (yellow)
4. A joint meeting of teacher, Department Chairman, and Director of Athletics will be set up where deemed necessary to discuss this observation.

From these observations, it is hoped that we can jointly work together to plan clinics, visitations, workshops, and individual help where needed.

It is essential that it be clearly understood that the main purpose of this observation form is to improve staff competencies.

Figure 3-1

PARMA PUBLIC SCHOOLS
DEPARTMENT OF ATHLETICS, PHYSICAL EDUCATION
AND RECREATION

OBSERVATION FORM

Teacher ______________________ Date ______________________

School ______________________ Subject ______________________

The prime object of this Observation Form is to serve as a constructive means of helping staff members to improve their teaching competencies.

Where deemed necessary, appropriate assistance or follow-up will be provided by the Director of Athletics, Physical Education and Recreation.

Desirable Qualities for Health and Physical Education Teachers
✔ = this item needs strengthening

I. Teaching Personality

Self control and poise.
Appropriate sense of humor.
Emotional stability.
Vitality and good health.
Enthusiasm in working with students
Appearance (neat and appropriate dress)
Punctuality in attendance.
Voice quality.
English usage (grammar)

II. Professional Qualities

Has harmonious relationship with other staff members.
Participates in staff meetings and discussions.
Upholds departmental and school policies, rules and regulations.
Follows planned prescribed program.
Cooperates with co-teachers and department chairman.
Willingness to assume extra duties.
Relationship with parents.
Written reports (on time and organized)

III. Class Management

Prompt in meeting class.
Supervises locker room before and after activity.
Makes maximum time available for instruction.
Utilizes every opportunity for instruction.
Demonstrates care of equipment and facilities.
Class discipline and control (based on respect not fear of reprisal.)
Utilization of student leaders as assistants (not in place of the teacher).
Commands respect by example in appearance, manners, behavior and language.

IV. Teaching Performance

Well versed in subject matter content.
Provides for individual as well as group instruction and activity.
Demonstrations to class kept to a minimum - keeps entire class active.
Recognizes individual differences and abilities.
Is sympathetic; fair, tolerant and patient with students.
Is well versed in and practices safety procedures.

V. Willing to serve on Physical Education Curriculum Committee. ____ Yes ____ No

VI. Constructive suggestions: ____

Completed by ______________________

Figure 3-2

The form shown in Figure 3-3 was devised by Mr. Bob James, director of athletics of the Warren, Michigan Consolidated Schools. This may be used in evaluating high school coaches. It can be used by the athletic director or by the coach as a self-evaluation checklist. This kind of professional evaluation gives the coach an opportunity to be informed about his strong points and his shortcomings.

This evaluation sheet appeared in the May 1970 issue of the "Athletic Director," which is a newsletter published by the National Council of Secondary School Athletic Directors, a council of the Division of Men's Athletics of the American Association for Health, Physical Education, and Recreation.

Name of Coach	Building		Assignment
DIRECTOR TO USE _X_ FOR RATING COACH TO USE _√_ FOR RATING			
	Below Average	*Average*	*Above Average*
1. PROFESSIONAL AND PERSONAL RELATIONSHIPS: a. Cooperation with building principal, faculty mgr. or department head in regard to submitting eligibility list, equipment needs, program information relative to your sport, etc.			
b. Rapport with coaching staff			
c. Appropriate dress at practices and games			
d. Participation in a reasonable number of professional and in-service meetings			
e. Public Relations: Cooperation with newspapers, radio, & T.V.			

Figure 3-3

	Below Average	*Average*	*Above Average*
f. Dad's night, team parties, banquets, outings, letters to colleges regarding players, service groups etc., encourage student to enter sports for the benefit of sports.			
g. Sideline conduct at games toward players, officials			
2. COACHING PERFORMANCE: a. Respect—sets example			
b. Supervision and Administration of locker and training room			
c. Knowledge of the sport			
d. Is innovative—uses new coaching techniques and ideas			
3. RELATED RESPONSIBILITIES: a. Compliance with meeting deadlines, inventory, equipment, preseason format, etc.			
b. Care of equipment, issue and storage			
c. Detail work for eligibility information & knowledge of state eligibility rules & sport rule changes			

4. RELATED INFORMATION:

a. Areas of strengths or weakness: ______________________

b. General comments or observations: ______________________

____

____

SIGNATURE OF DIRECTOR______________________

SIGNATURE OF COACH______________________

Date______________________

We have considered evaluation of the athletic program and of the athletic staff as it pertains to teaching and coaching. It might be well to reflect on some of the major areas that administrators, coaches, parents, and other citizens of the community deem important in evaluating the director of athletics. A similar list may be devised by any of these groups and may also be useful in hiring a new director of athletics.

1. Is he a good organizer and a good supervisor?
2. Does he take a genuine interest in all phases of the program?
3. Are the relations good with other schools, officials, police, physicians, etc.
4. Is the rapport good with the administration, coaching staff, other faculty members and parents.
5. Is he really a professional educator?
6. Does he communicate well?
7. Are his qualities such that he is a competent representative of the school system?

Many other questions can be asked, but answers to these can tell an interesting story.

FOUR

Developing Persuasive Public Relations with Parents and Community

More and more stress is being placed on the importance of a sound public relations program in every phase of every field. Athletics is certainly no exception. We have a golden opportunity to really sell our program to more people than any other facet of education. Yet we frequently "miss the boat" and fail to take advantage of considerable opportunities in public relations matters.

This chapter offers many suggestions which can help create a favorable image in developing an interscholastic athletic program.

DEALINGS WITH PRESS, RADIO AND TELEVISION

Prompt Communication

Oftentimes an athletic director is overwhelmed by requests by local and area newspapers. These may take the form of schedules, team rosters, information on special nights, coaching assignments, etc. There is a tendency to minimize the importance of these requests by failing to return necessary information to the papers or by slipshod, inaccurate reporting.

These requests must receive prompt attention and should not be referred to the coach of a particular sport unless the matter deals specifically with his team members. Coaches are busy with the details of game preparations and may tend to procrastinate or minimize the significance of prompt and accurate communication.

Student Reporters

The employment of students in reporting scores and game details is a highly recommended procedure. Students must be carefully screened and selected since they are representatives of the school. It is most important that they be knowledgeable, accurate, and reliable.

These reporters are paid by the news media rather than the school. The athletic director should work closely with these students so that they have the necessary guidance in dealing with the press, radio, and television stations.

Special Consideration

Most schools make an honest effort to be hospitable to representatives of the news media at games, banquets, assemblies, etc. Prior arrangements should also be made to invite these men by letter or by telephone to other special events as well.

A reserved section in the press box at football games and a special section near the scoring table in basketball games and wrestling matches should be set aside for this purpose. Game programs, statistics sheets, and other similar data should be made available to these reporters.

At athletic banquets the news media representatives should be seated at the head table or at a special place near the head table. They should be introduced with the other special guests and thanked for their cooperation and interest in the program. Sometimes they may serve as masters of ceremonies or speakers at banquets or other special affairs.

The direct, as well as indirect, involvement of these men in the athletic program is beneficial to all aspects of the school system.

A set policy pertaining to news releases as they pertain to the athletic program are important. This policy should be uniform in each building and should be carefully followed. Such a plan can avoid confusion, overlapping, and embarrassment.

COOPERATION WITH LOCAL SERVICE CLUBS

Local service clubs are most vital in promoting youth activities at all age levels. The involvement of these organizations in promoting the athletic program follows naturally. Since the cooperation of the service clubs and the athletic department is most significant, several guidelines should be followed.

1. All requests for funds, for assistance with projects, etc. will be made through the director of athletics. This avoids many problems and reflects good organization.
2. Offer assistance to local service clubs on their projects. Help them with promotion as well as manpower.
3. Make the coaches, the athletes, and yourself (the director of athletics) available for talks, programs, etc.
4. Join a club if at all possible and be an active member. Encourage your staff to do likewise.
5. Have written policies and procedures to follow for each project undertaken. An example of this guideline follows.

Each year the Berea, Ohio, Kiwanis Club helps sponsor the Berea Relays. This is a large invitational track meet involving twenty-four schools. The management of a meet of this type requires much work and organization. The part that a sponsoring club plays should be clearly spelled out.

The following are the policies and procedures for the Berea Kiwanis Club in this project.

Duties and Responsibilities of the Berea Kiwanis Club in Co-Sponsoring Annual Berea Relays Track and Field Meet

The following suggestions may serve as a guide line for the Boys and Girls Committee Chairmen of the Berea Kiwanis Club in regard to the sponsoring of the Annual Berea Relays.

1. To obtain sponsors for the various trophies that are given at the Berea Relays. Championship and Runner-up trophies are awarded each year in addition to twelve trophies for the various relays events. The donation by each sponsor is $15.00, which will more than cover the cost of the trophies. The difference in the cost of the trophies and

the donation is usually $3.00, which will apply on the purchase of medals and ribbons for this meet.

2. The profits of the concession stand will be given to the Berea Kiwanis Club to help offset this payment.
3. The $150.00 in the Berea Kiwanis budget for this event should be sufficient to cover the balance of expenses for these awards. If these expenses should exceed the $150.00 allotted, the Berea High Athletic Association will make up the difference.
4. Each year several of the Berea Kiwanians are interested in serving as officials at this track meet. They are more than welcome to help if they are interested. The Boys and Girls Committee Chairman should forward the list of these men to the meet manager in sufficient time for program printing.
5. None of the officials are paid for working at this meet. Each official will, however, be given a cap, which he may keep. The expenses for the purchase of these caps will be defrayed by the Berea High Athletic Association.
6. Any publicity which the Berea Kiwanis Club can give on this project will be greatly appreciated.
7. Members of the Berea Kiwanis Club will be admitted free of charge to this meet by proper identification at the gate.

Guest Nights

One of the very best public relations projects that the athletic department can undertake is to have special nights whereby service club members and their families are guests. This may be done in football, basketball, wrestling, or swimming, provided the seating capacity is adequate. Games or meets which draw capacity crowds should be avoided for such programs.

Special invitations to the club presidents should be mailed sufficiently in advance of the designated night. Definite instructions for admission, seating, etc. must be included. Public address announcements introducing these guests as a group is very effective.

A typical letter to a local service club is shown in Figure 4-1.

Mr. Will Nopper
President of Berea Rotary Club
341 Crossbrook Drive
Berea, Ohio 44017

Dear Mr. Nopper:

Saturday, January 19, has been designated as Berea Rotary Night for the home Berea High basketball game with Fairview Park High School. The junior varsity game will begin at 7:00 p.m. and the varsity game will start at approximately 8:30 p.m.

Halftime entertainment is being furnished by the gymnastics club.

For admission to the game, your members may identify themselves with their regular membership cards. We will be looking forward to seeing you and the other Rotarians that evening.

Thanks once again for your cooperation in our various school projects.

Sincerely,

Bob Purdy
Athletic Director

Figure 4-1

Co-Sponsor Banquets

One of the very best projects that any service club can help sponsor are high school athletics banquets. There are many different ways to organize these affairs. There are also many different ways to involve these local clubs.

Probably the best approach is to invite the club president or one of his representatives to a planning meeting. If other sponsoring groups are taking part in this program, such as the boosters club, they too should have someone representing them at the meeting. The director of athletics should chair this meeting and have a well structured agenda prepared.

Most of the banquet details should be handled by the director of athletics. The service clubs should be responsible for ticket sales to their own membership, any publicity their group may wish to arrange, and have a small part in the program such as a short welcome talk.

These clubs often help subsidize the cost of these banquets by flat, predetermined donations.

ACTIVE PARTICIPATION IN BOOSTERS CLUB

Close Cooperation on Boosters Club Projects

The director of athletics and members of his staff must be willing to cooperate with the school boosters club on their money raising projects. Some of these activities are time consuming while others are more of an organizational type function.

How can we really do our part in the limited amount of time that we have available?

1. Work at spaghetti and pancake dinners.
2. Make facilities available for program sales, concession stand operation, etc.
3. Have student team members available for car parking responsibility.
4. Cooperate in ticket sales for boosters club projects.
5. Make contacts for program advertisements, patrons' listings, etc.
6. Help publicize boosters club programs and activities.

Football Film

One of the best public relations activities that we have conducted at our high schools has been Thursday evening football film sessions. The program consists of movies of last week's junior varsity and varsity football games. These are narrated by the coaches, with certain plays being explained and questions answered.

The coaches who do the scouting then give a report on the opponent in this weeks game. This also proves to be very interesting.

Announcements are given on such matters as ticket sales, spectator buses for away games, boosters club projects, homecoming, etc.

The program is concluded with a coffee hour and informal discussions with the parents. These meetings are well attended and are greatly appreciated by parents, boosters members, and other interested people in the community.

Appreciation Projects

In appreciation for the assistance given by the boosters club in helping with the many athletic events, the director of athletics and his staff should reciprocate in different ways.

The sale of adult season tickets at reduced prices is always well accepted by boosters club members, parents, service clubs, etc. Seating of these groups in special reserved sections is also very popular.

Boosters club nights at home winter sports events are excellent ways to express thanks to these people. They may be granted free admission by showing their membership cards. Refreshments may also be served following these games.

One of the best ways of showing appreciation is by sending "thank you" letters to committee chairmen and club officers following a successful project. Many of the boosters club members spend considerable time at these activities and greatly deserve these letters.

Special awards to key people who have done outstanding work should be given at the athletic banquets or awards assemblies.

Special Nights Honoring Parents

Many athletic departments have parents' nights in football, basketball, wrestling, and swimming. Letters inviting the parents to these games should be mailed sufficiently early to help avoid conflicts. The parents of cheerleaders, managers, statisticians, and others connected with the program should also be included.

A typical letter of invitation is shown in Figure 4-2.

Parents' nights near the end of the season are always well received. Pre-season programs for parents are equally important. This is an excellent opportunity for the coaches to meet the parents and for the parents to meet each other.

The coach can use this occasion to display equipment used in practice and games, to explain training rules and regulations, to encourage parental cooperation in academic courses, to introduce squad members, and to demonstrate drills used in practice sessions.

Date

Dear Parents:

We are setting aside Friday, November 11, for our annual Parents' Night game. Midpark plays host to a very good St. Edward team in our final home varsity football game.

We should like to have all the parents of players, cheerleaders, and managers present, if at all possible. This year, we will have a special section reserved, with Mothers and Dads sitting together in the stands. The Dads will be given numbers that correspond to their son's numbers. The mothers will be given mums. Please pick these up on the track in front of the stands. If possible, we would like to have you present by 7:45 P.M. for introductions.

This letter will serve as your admission ticket for both parents to the game.

We greatly appreciate your interest and cooperation in our athletic program and are looking forward to seeing you at the game.

Sincerely,

Bob Purdy
Director of Athletics

Dick Lowry
Football Coach

Figure 4-2

When the players have survived the final cut and the squad has been selected, the coach should send a letter to the parents of the team members. This is significant even if there are pre-season programs for parents.

An example of such a letter follows:

Dear Parents:

Congratulations! Your son is a member of the Ford Junior High Basketball team for the coming season. To him this is an honor and a privilege. I am sure that through his participation in this activity many benefits will be derived, besides acquiring basketball skills. The chance to be a member of a group of his peers, and to be looked up to by other boys and girls, are strong desires and needs of youth of this age.

Since your son is representing Ford Junior High School, I expect his cooperation in the following: He should make every effort to keep his grades at the level of his previous averages and, if possible, strive to improve them; when we travel to other schools we expect him to wear a sport coat, shirt and tie; he must adhere without exception to the following rules of health: No smoking, maintenance of an adequate diet and a healthy sleeping schedule, and in general discipline himself in such a manner as to be a good citizen in school, as well as being a good student.

I believe that if your boy follows these rules, he will be personally rewarded through his efforts for the next four months. I hope that he will develop many commendable characteristics and habits which will lead to a more fruitful life as well as to being a better basketball player. It is important that every teenager learn how to win and how to lose, because he will be facing the problems of the adult world in a few short years. Nowhere else in his school life is this challenge so real as on the athletic field. I believe playing on the Ford Junior High basketball team is a real opportunity in regard to this challenge. I am certain that your son will benefit from it.

Our practice time will be late due to intramurals and the late hour of school closing time. We will practice each evening until 6:15. The boys should be showered and ready to leave the building no later than 6:30 p.m. I realize that this is not the most *ideal* hour, but it allows little more than one hour and thirty minutes in which to practice.

Basketball is considered an extra-curricular activity and should by no means interfere with the regular school curriculum. If your son is unable to meet requirements we expect of him, then we suggest he drop basketball.

I apologize in advance to you mothers who will face the problems of late meals, transportation, and the dozen or so other inconveniences which will occur during this basketball season. I feel certain, however, that when it is concluded you will feel that the experience was more than worthwhile for your son.

Sincerely,

Head Basketball Coach,
Ford Junior High School

General Procedures

To be really successful, any public relations program must have definite aims and objectives. There must also be specific goals. There must be an honest effort to include all of the staff members and squad members, to be aware of these goals, and to work toward their fulfillment.

The display of good sportsmanship both on and off the field is vital. This includes all of the people participating in the program. There is really no place for young men and women in the program unless they are willing to conduct themselves as good citizens.

Many schools receive a good or bad reputation from the actions and reactions of their athletic teams and coaches. As representatives of schools and communities we must constantly be aware of our responsibilities and obligations. The behavior of student spectators, cheerleaders, and adult followers is also a definite reflection on the school and the athletic program being conducted.

The use of special cheering sections may help promote school spirit as well as good sportsmanship. Senior men's clubs, pep clubs, and similar organizations can be very helpful if they are properly organized and supervised.

The strength or weakness characterized by the athletic program goes a long way in helping to determine the kind of school that we have. The spirit, enthusiasm, and attitude of the student body and community carry over into other activities and into the curriculum as well. Success and failure are both very contagious. We naturally prefer success, which is actually the end result of a good program.

Every organization and association should have a code of ethics and then adhere to it. Such a program for ethical behavior is important in all activities. Codes of ethics as they apply to state and national organizations are discussed in Chapter Sixteen.

If a public relations program is to succeed, we must undertake each project with a positive attitude. We are constantly selling our program with constructive efforts.

Mr. Charles Moser, Athletic Director of the Abilene, Texas Public Schools, has incorporated many excellent ideas in the athletic department of that system. His philosophy of public relations in athletics is that of helping other people. This is quite refreshing since the attitude of many people is, "Who can I get to help *me?*" If we are interested in assisting others, it is amazing how many people are interested in our welfare.

Mr. Moser's plan to honor a teacher of the year from their secondary schools is most worthwhile. The teacher selected for this award is one who has shown a real interest in the athletic program for that particular year. It is based on attendance at games and general involvement in the program. Mr. Moser finds that this has greatly improved the relationship between the athletic department and the other members of the teaching staff. The recipient for this award is chosen by members of the athletic teams. The presentation is made at a regular athletic awards assembly.

The Abilene High Schools also honor a member of the boosters club each week. A name is pulled from a hat to determine who accompanies the team. This person goes with the squad on the team bus, has his meals with the team, has locker room privileges, etc. Undertakings such as these help our adult constituents to better appreciate and understand the athletic program.

The cooperation of the athletic director, coaches, and players with the custodians is most important. Special care should be taken in locking doors, turning off showers, care of equipment, being careful not to bring in mud, etc. We must attempt to help these men rather than use them.

A close association and working relationship between the administration, board of education, and the athletic department is most important. The coaches and teachers must work closely together on discipline and eligibility problems. A successful public relations program for the athletic department needs the cooperation of all board of education employees.

We should be willing to cooperate with the other departments of the school. We can do much to encourage participation by students in attendance at their programs, and sharing facilities and equipment.

The athletic director and coaches can do much to assist the senior athletes in obtaining college scholarships and in helping them to select the proper schools. There is much need to properly guide these young men as to future committments. The coaches can often assist the guidance counselors in helping give direction to students other than athletes.

One of the most important times to display our interest and concern for young people may be during the summer months. During this time they drift away from our control and association and may tend to run into real problems. We in turn can help by assisting them with summer employment and by attendance at basketball and wrestling camps or similar activities. Enrollment in summer school may also prove to be beneficial.

The summer is also a good time for us to make personal visits on parents who recently moved into the community. We can acquaint them and their son with our program, policies, and general procedures. In turn we can encourage him to participate and help him to know other team members before school begins in the fall.

The summer also provides us with an opportunity to meet with parents of students who have had eligibility or discipline problems. People are generally more relaxed at this time of the year and solutions to these problems can often be more readily solved.

Although the care and treatment of injuries to athletes is covered in another chapter of this book, the public relations value is most significant. This is an area where we can do much to sell our program.

The athletic director and coaches can greatly improve relationships with parents by sending them letters of congratulations for the outstanding achievements of their son. Parents and relatives greatly appreciate cards or flowers sent by the athletic department when a member of the family expires or becomes seriously ill.

FIVE

Financing a Productive Interscholastic Program on any Budget

Every school and every athletic department has a wide variety of problems and concerns that vary with the size of the school, the size of the program, the kind of support received from the student body and the community, the success of the teams, and many other things.

One problem that seems to have an almost universal and continuous effect on every athletic department, from the smallest high school to the largest university, is that of properly financing the program.

The chapter illustrates a sound business approach in dealing with the many facets of the financial problem in athletics.

ROLE OF THE BOOSTERS CLUB

One of the most important sources of financial assistance to any high school athletic department is the Boosters Club. The question should not be "Do we need?" or "Should we have?" such an organization. The question is rather what type of group shall we have and how will it best function.

The object of such an organization should be to foster and promote the interest of the local citizens in the various co-curricular activities participated in by the students of that particular school, and to cooperate with members of the faculty and school authorities in the furtherance of education and recreation.

Some athletic directors may not agree with the philosophy of having a boosters club function to assist other co-curricular groups in addition to athletics. The largest portion of this budget should be earmarked for athletics. But if we are to gain the status that we want, and then hope to maintain this status, it will be necessary for us to constantly make every effort to keep our athletic program in the "mainstream" of the entire school curriculum, which is exactly where it belongs.

In working with booster's clubs there are four major points that must be resolved in financial assistance. First, since the vast majority of the income received by the Boosters Club is derived from athletic related events, the larger portion of the revenue should go to athletics. Second, the actual allocation of the money as to respective teams and projects shall be the decision of the principal and athletic director and not the Boosters Club executive board. This will eliminate many problems caused by "well-meaning" people who might designate monies for projects of less importance and need than others. Since the school administrators and coaches know the problems far better, they should be responsible for disbursement of the funds. Third, all sports should benefit from this money. This may be done by applying the funds to assist in transportation for all teams, an equipment fund affecting all teams, or similar projects. Since every sport is important, each one should receive monies. Fourth, no coach should be permitted to request funds for his particular sport from the Boosters Club. This is most important because of the many problems that can result. Each coach feels his sport is most important and that his needs must be met. If this practice is permitted, bedlam will prevail. The Boosters Club will not know which coach has the most pressing request. The Boosters Club must cooperate with this policy at all times.

A suggested ratio to show receipts for all sports as donated by the Boosters Club is as follows:

Football	28%
Cheerleaders	4%
Cross Country	4%
Basketball	18%
Swimming	10%
Wrestling	10%
Track	10%
Baseball	8%
Golf	4%
Tennis	4%
Total	100%

Listed in Figure 5-1 is a Boosters Club budget which indicates receipts and expenditures for an entire school year. You will notice that athletics does receive the major part of the disbursement through direct donation, athletic banquets, etc. You will also notice that many other groups share in these disbursements. Although Midpark is a rather large high school, similar budgets may be adopted for schools of different sizes.

This is a very sound policy since many different groups benefit, and considerably more parental and teacher interest and cooperation is shown. Midpark High School has an enrollment of 1900 in grades 10-12.

MIDPARK HIGH SCHOOL

Budget for the Year 19x5-19x6

INCOME:

Memberships	$ 114.00
Patrons	1,620.00
Professional Patrons	320.00
Advertising	7,035.00
Parking Lot	380.00
Program Sales	700.00
Athletic Banquets	750.00
Scholarship Banquet	400.00
Profit from Dinner Dance	500.00
Profit from Spaghetti Dinner	1,850.00
Profit—Wrestling Weekends	800.00
Popcorn—Basketball, Wrestling	370.00

Sale of old popcorn machine	150.00
Profit from Home Days	105.00
Miscellaneous	150.00
Total Income	$15,244.00

EXPENSES:

Athletics

Athletic Banquets	$ 1,350.00
Injuries	100.00
Printing of Programs	2,500.00
Team Pictures	100.00
Athletic Assoc. (donation)	4,500.00
Parking Expense–Police	170.00
Raincoats for Parking	84.00
Oranges for Football and Wrestling Teams	75.00
Autographed Footballs	46.00
Basketballs	77.00

Music:

Band	$ 2,000.00
Choral Department	1,000.00

Other

Postage, Stationery and Printing	150.00
Refreshments	25.00
English Department Publication	150.00
School Paper	200.00
Yearbook	250.00
Scholarship Awards	200.00
Scholarship Banquet	750.00
Exchange Student Program	100.00
Graphic Arts Activities	200.00
Teacher Appreciation Day	15.00
New Teacher Coffee	25.00
Boys' and Girls' State	105.00
Popcorn Supplies	125.00
New Teacher Luncheon	25.00
Art Department	225.00
Junior Achievements Program	43.00
Future Teachers of America	50.00

Post Prom Committee	200.00
Key Chains	190.00
Miscellaneous	214.00
Total Expenses	$15,244.00

Figure 5-1

As is usually the case, this club has a fairly large membership but only about twenty hard workers.

INVOLVEMENT OF THE BOARD OF EDUCATION

In all states except Iowa and Washington, the boards of education are given legal power to use public tax monies to help support athletic and other activities. This will vary greatly by state and by school boards within each state. In all cases the use of these funds is at the discretion of the local boards of education and is not of a mandatory nature.

Ohio was the last state to pass such legislation. This is especially significant since the bill, from its very inception, was spearheaded by the Ohio High School Athletic Directors Association. Nelson Thinnes, Athletic Director at Cincinnati Aiken High School, was president of the state athletic directors association; Rex Smith, Athletic Director of the Parma City Schools was legislative chairman, and Robert Purdy, vice-president of the association. These three were largely responsible for this bill being enacted on December 11, 1967.

One of the most significant features of legislation of this type is that it enables areas such as interscholastic athletics to be given similar privileges as other parts of the school curriculum. This is one goal which all athletic directors seem to be constantly working toward.

The question is, how can we involve the boards of education in such a way that they may be of real financial assistance to the athletic program and at the same time will not alienate the average taxpayer? There are many schools of thought on this question but the following areas seem to be quite educationally sound.

First, we should approach this problem keeping safety in mind. Have the boards of education consider the payment of bus transportation for all teams and bands. They should also be willing to help with police protection bills, and those of medical doctors in attendance at all football games and other large athletic events involving four or more schools. Most taxpayers and even some board of education members might think they are subsidizing this part of the program even if they are not. These figures would represent approximately twenty percent of the annual budget.

Second, don't get involved in purchasing cloth goods or similar equipment. This can be a curse for obvious reasons and tend to alienate the board members and citizens alike. Safety items, such as those mentioned above, can easily be defended.

Third, the use of board of education funds may greatly assist in financing programs when new senior or junior high schools are opened. The tremendous drain on existing schools to help new ones to open is unbelievable.

Fourth, many times schools are forced to overschedule their teams, particularly in football, in order to receive large guarantees that help finance the program. Trends such as this could be greatly reduced or eliminated by board of education funds.

Fifth, with additional monies new sports could be added to the program and more boys carried on existing teams.

Sixth, school athletic departments could avoid some of the very ridiculous money raising projects that are now so prevalent. This is not to imply by any means that athletic sponsored drives for funds should be eliminated. It could, however, help to curb many educationally unsound promotions, such as raffles and other gimmicks.

ASSISTANCE OF SERVICE CLUBS

Most service clubs are looking for worthwhile projects in their respective communities. School connected activities usually rank near the top of their list.

In dealing with service clubs, as in boosters clubs, there should be a central clearinghouse for requests at the school, in order to avoid a real problem. Since groups other than athletic teams are constantly seeking financial assistance, the principal, athletic director, and other activity sponsors should meet periodically to help funnel these requests into a more orderly fashion.

Here again it is best to avoid asking assistance in purchasing uniforms and similar equipment. There will be sufficient money for these items in the school's athletic fund when other needs can be handled elsewhere.

Most service clubs to which I have belonged seemed most receptive to such projects as trophies for invitational relay meets in track, holiday wrestling tournament awards, co-sponsoring athletic banquets with other service clubs and the Boosters Club, partially subsidizing cheerleaders to summer camps, etc. Since the officers, directors, and committee chairmen of these clubs change each year, it is wise for the school to make the same or similar requests from one year to the next for best results.

Although most service clubs are more than willing to cooperate with school athletic departments, they may not always be financially sound themselves. These things are important to know when making requests.

SPECIAL MONEY RAISING PROJECTS

Each year boosters clubs and athletic departments conduct many and varied forms of money raising projects. These depend in part on the community and on what type of drives have been successful in the past.

Several important points must be stressed for maximum and lasting results. First, emphasis should be placed on a limited number of projects for the athletic department during a given school year. These undertakings should not exceed three each year and should be spaced at different times of the year.

Second, the dates for these projects should be set early and should be coordinated with the major boosters club events which should also be limited in number.

Third, all of the coaches, regardless of their sports, should take an active part in these drives. This tends to give a much more unified effort, plus the needed manpower to get the job done.

Fourth, we must be well organized. A competent chairman is a must. The various assignments and sub-committees must be clearly spelled out as to specific duties and responsibilities. Good publicity; pre-sale of tickets, and advance planning will help insure success for these affairs.

Fifth, it is important to give the people something for their money. Many people buy tickets to benefit basketball games, pancake dinners, and similar projects and never use these tickets.

However, if they do attend that function, they should not be disappointed.

Even though boosters clubs, service clubs, and boards of education are anxious to assist athletic departments financially, they are even more inclined to cooperate if they see that we are willing to help ourselves.

In referring back to the boosters club budget you will notice that there are three main fund raising drives. In the late spring and early summer, advertisements and patrons' listings are sold for the football and basketball programs. In November, a big spaghetti dinner is held, at which time nearly 2500 people are fed. In February a dinner-dance is sponsored. It has also been highly successful. These are the only special fund raising projects which they hold. They are highly successful since they are well planned and since considerable effort is put forth in a soundly coordinated manner.

Athletic departments can make substantial profits from pancake dinners, candy drives, Christmas tree sales, etc. Two of the most successful ventures in my estimation are door-to-door ticket drives and slave days.

Football ticket drives conducted in late August by members of the team prove highly successful. This should include not only football players, but cheerleaders, band members, and cross-country men. They should canvass the district in cars driven by adults, and be dressed in their athletic uniforms. Refreshments for all participating and prizes for the top salesmen and highest car totals add more incentive to this project. The citizens are very receptive to this sort of drive and often begin to attend games that they ordinarily would not.

Slave days are most popular in the spring. The athletic director should select a Saturday not too heavily booked with athletic events. All of the boys and girls on teams should participate. They may either get their own jobs or be assigned jobs by their coaches. Boys usually wash screens, clean out garages, rake yards, etc. Girls may baby-sit or do routine housework. The students should be expected to work a half day and should turn over their earnings to the athletic department. Those not having specific jobs should conduct a car wash at the school at the same time. This project is also well received by the community and students, and can be very profitable.

PHYSICAL EDUCATION DEPARTMENT BUDGET

In many instances the physical education department can allocate a portion of their budget for certain items to be used by the athletic department. This will vary greatly with school systems and with the policy governing these appropriations.

Such items as first aid equipment, balls, nets for tennis and basketball, mats for wrestling, etc., are often purchased and can be used for both physical education and athletic department programs.

Since these things are purchased from board of education monies, this offers further relief from purchasing directly from athletic department funds.

RESPONSIBILITY OF THE ATHLETIC ASSOCIATION

Although considerable assistance in financing an interscholastic athletic program may come from a number of sources already mentioned in this chapter, the major responsibility lies within the framework of the athletic association itself. Probably no one area comes under more discussion or creates more problems than the establishment of a proper budget.

Since the average coach and many athletic directors are not as familiar as they should be with good business procedures, the problem becomes even greater. Most coaches feel that their job is one of coaching and not of financial planning or wise spending. There is often the feeling on their part that this is not their problem, but that whatever equipment they need should be purchased.

In order to get properly organized, a preliminary meeting of all head coaches, the principal, faculty manager, and athletic director should be held in January each year. This meeting should be of a general nature to acquaint each coach with what is expected of him in preparing a budget. He should have a format or some specific guidelines to follow.

Individual sessions should be held with each head coach following the preliminary meeting to assist them with problems pertinent to their particular sport. A second general meeting should be held about two weeks later to submit the budgets and to discuss items of major importance.

The budget should then be reviewed by the athletic director, faculty manager, and principal. Certain items may be deleted and others added before final approval is given. The needs for some larger and more expensive equipment and cost increases in many areas should be considered.

Copies of the final budget should be made available to all coaches and other school personnel involved in the athletic program as well as the principal, the superintendent, and the board of education. This removes all doubts and suspicions concerning approved items for all concerned.

The final amounts for each sport should depend on an anticipated income for the entire school year. It is also recommended that each sport be given a certain percentage of this total. The reason for meeting in January to set up budgets for the following school year is to enable the football coach to have several months leaway in ordering equipment for the fall.

Figure 5-2 is a face-sheet for Midpark High School's athletic budget. Schools of all sizes should prepare athletic association budgets and financial statements. Amounts may vary but a proper business-like approach is most important.

MIDPARK HIGH SCHOOL

Athletic Association Budget
19x5-19x6

	Anticipated Income
Football	$14,000.00
Basketball	6,000.00
Wrestling	1,700.00
Swimming	1,000.00
Boosters Club	2,000.00
Special Projects	2,000.00
	$26,700.00

	Budget Expenditures
Football	$10,723.50
Cross-Country	335.00
Basketball	2,972.00
Wrestling	1,625.00

Swimming	1,325.00
Golf	475.00
Track	1,355.00
Tennis	542.00
Baseball	1,060.00
Cheerleaders	490.00
Jr. High Program	1,000.00
Girls' Program	100.00
Total	$22,003.00

Figure 5-2

Figure 5-3 is an example of the football budget for Midpark High School. Each sport listed on the face-sheet would be similar in content.

MIDPARK HIGH FOOTBALL BUDGET 19x5-19x6

Equipment	$ 4,390.00
Special Police	96.00
Gate Help	252.00
Officials	360.00
Injuries	100.00
Printing	50.00
Cleaning	480.00
Scouting	300.00
Films	1,400.00
Reconditioning	2,000.00
League Dues	85.00
Miscellaneous	150.00
Tape	240.00
Warren Harding Trip	210.00
Clinics	400.00
Awards	210.00
Total	$10,723.50

Special note—No transportation, city police, or doctors' fees for attending games are shown. These costs are defrayed by the board of education.

Figure 5-3

FOOTBALL EQUIPMENT

1 Brek Timer	$ 100.00
12 Helmets, (big masks)	350.00
12 Shoulder pads (4 big hitter, QB pad)	240.00
20 Hip pads	250.00
48 Practice jerseys (warm)	160.00
50 Practice pants ($6.00 per pair)	300.00
20 Pair arm pads	100.00
15 Pairs hand pads	30.00
2 Knee braces	20.00
1 Training kit (double shoe laces, pad laces)	100.00
6 Footballs (game)	120.00
6 Pair knee pads	15.00
150 Mouth guards	200.00
5 pairs coaching pants	70.00
40 Pairs game pants	400.00
45 Game jerseys (white)	430.00
10 Game jerseys (brown)	180.00
72 Tee shirts (football)	120.00
20 Pairs thigh guards	90.00
1 Tackleback sled	350.00
60 Nylon mesh jerseys	225.00
60 Tassel caps	135.00
50 Duffle bags	250.00
2 Stand up dummies	70.00
2 Sled pads (7 man)	60.00
2 Rolls stripping tape and awards	25.00
Total	$4,390.00

Figure 5-3 *(continued)*

ANNUAL FINANCIAL REPORT

At the conclusion of each school year the athletic director or the person responsible for the business affairs at the high school should prepare an annual financial report. This should reflect all of the income and expenses and should be costed or charged to each sport. In this manner clear and accurate insight is gained as to the actual financial status of the athletic department.

Although the final report is not available until June or July of each year, it is most important to be costing and itemizing these accounts every few days. By compiling this annual report, it is easy to compare with items on the budgets and to determine if we are realistic in our estimates and planning.

Copies of this report (as the budget) should be made available to all coaches, the principal, the superintendent of schools, the board of education, and other school personnel involved in the athletic program.

Figure 5-4 is a sample of the face-sheet of the annual report for Berea High School in Berea, Ohio. Also shown is the basketball report, which is similar to that of the other sports.

Berea High School has an enrollment of 1400 students.

BEREA HIGH SCHOOL ATHLETIC ASSOCIATION
Financial Report 19x5-19x6
July 21, 19x6

	Receipts	*Expenditures*
Opening Balances (deficit)		$ 8,514.64
*Administrative	$15,582.11	8,889.19
Football	13,790.24	9,807.25
Cross Country	32.00	322.95
Basketball	6,788.74	3,476.74
Swimming	1,068.97	1,464.06
Wrestling	999.06	1,578.28
Track	670.65	1,359.91
Baseball	17.30	527.95
Golf	7.00	247.30
Tennis	6.70	150.77
Cheerleaders	674.06	1,166.74
Band		
Total	$39,636.83	$37,505.78

Balance–7/21/69-$2,131.05

* The administrative account includes such things as money received and spent on student and adult spectator buses, basketball tournament tickets, athletic banquet ticket sales, and similar items where money is received and shortly thereafter disbursed.

Figure 5-4

BASKETBALL REPORT

Receipts		*Expenditures*	
Mayfield Gate	457.00	½ Analyst Projector	212.50
Midpark Gate	392.90	Tournament Scouting	105.00
Maple Gate	398.50	Regional Tournament Expense Draw	650.00
Bay Gate	390.25	Complimentary Tournament Tickets	168.00
Rocky River Gate	370.56	Mileage to Drawing Banquets	17.30
Willoughby South Gate	293.02	Officials	139.00
Eastlake North Gate	426.00	Gate Help	190.00
Bedford Gate	264.74	Police	250.58
Mentor Gate	325.90	Equipment	44.34
Presale (Student)	416.57	Transportation	158.63
Elementary Ticket Sale	166.14	Film, Filming	648.00
Programs	219.96	Scouting	173.00
Season Tickets	217.00	Cleaning	233.95
Received–Sectional Tournament	399.23	Printing	50.00
Received–District Tournament	1,210.96	Supplies	34.44
Received–Regional Tournament	652.50	P.A., Scorer, Timer, Programs	270.00
Regional Tournament Expense Draw returned to fund	182.50	Clinics	45.00
Reimbursement from Student Council for Dance–Police	5.00	Awards	87.00
	$6,788.74		$3,476.00

Figure 5-5

PURCHASE ORDER

A purchase order similar to the one shown below is most important in the day-to-day operation of any athletic program.

The athletic director should insist that purchase orders be used and signed by the head coach in that particular sport. All suppliers should also be advised in writing that equipment bought and not properly processed by purchase orders will not be honored.

In emergencies it is necessary to phone orders to suppliers, but the proper paper work should follow. Such business practices can eliminate confusion as to prices quoted to athletic directors and coaches and those that later appear on invoices that are received.

Another distinct advantage in purchase orders is to remove any doubt as to what sport should be charged with each purchase. It also is very helpful in auditing the books.

For best results there should be five copies of a purchase order–1) to the supplier; 2) to the principal; 3) to the athletic director; 4) to the coach, and 5) to the bookkeeper.

Shown in Figure 5-6 is a Purchase Order for Berea High School Athletic Association.

MONTHLY REPORTS

It is very helpful if short monthly financial reports are made available during the school year. These should reflect the various income and expense items and should show the balance of the athletic association account at that time. Any unpaid bills should also be listed on this report.

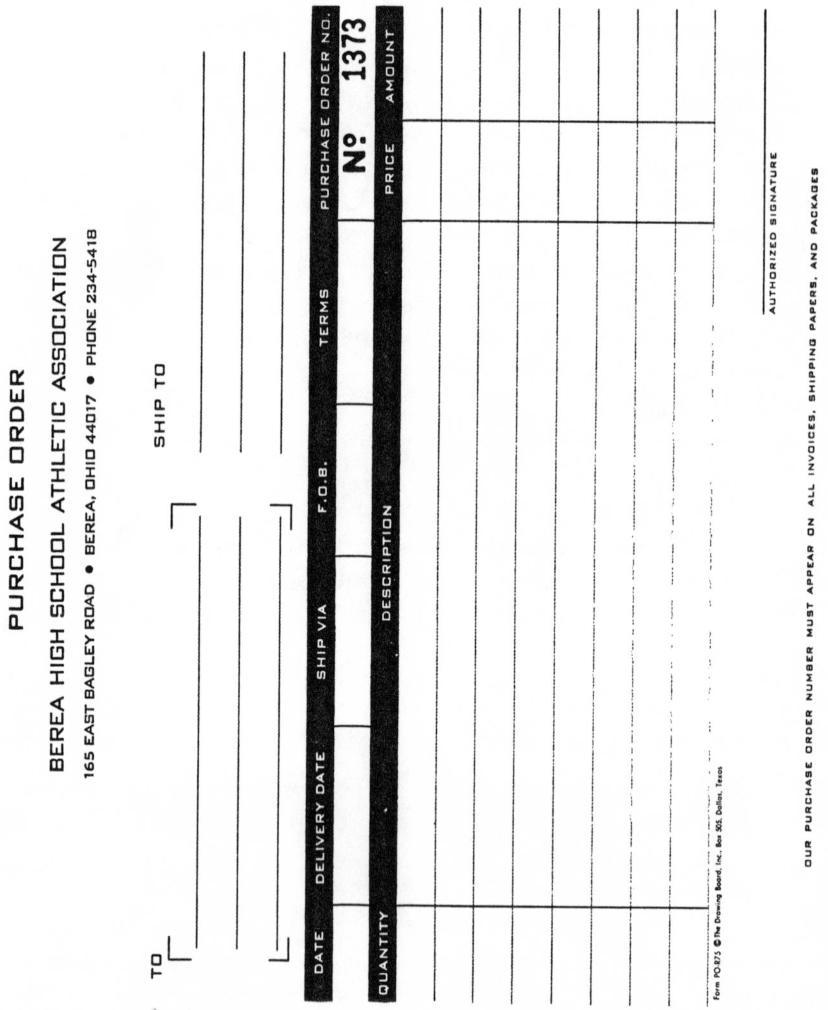

PURCHASE ORDER

BEREA HIGH SCHOOL ATHLETIC ASSOCIATION

165 EAST BAGLEY ROAD • BEREA, OHIO 44017 • PHONE 234-5418

TO

SHIP TO

DATE	DELIVERY DATE	SHIP VIA	F.O.B.	TERMS	PURCHASE ORDER NO.
					Nº 1373

QUANTITY	DESCRIPTION	PRICE	AMOUNT

Form PO-R75 © The Drawing Board, Inc., Box 505, Dallas, Texas

AUTHORIZED SIGNATURE

OUR PURCHASE ORDER NUMBER MUST APPEAR ON ALL INVOICES, SHIPPING PAPERS, AND PACKAGES

Figure 5-6

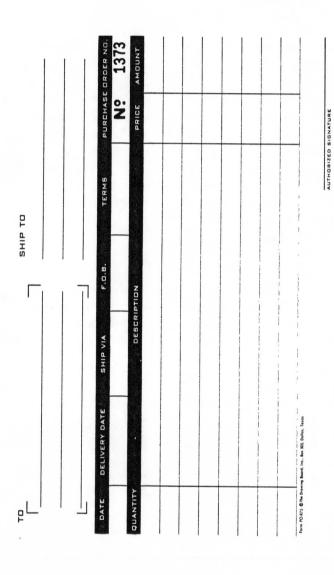

SIX

Building and Sustaining a Harmonious Physical Education and Intramural Program

The development of a sound athletic program should be complemented by an equally good physical education and intramural program. This chapter deals with the latter two phases and with the necessary cooperation between all three departments.

DEVELOPMENT OF A SENIOR HIGH SCHOOL PHYSICAL EDUCATION PROGRAM

Physical education is an activity-centered body of knowledge which has as its aim the development of physically, mentally, morally, emotionally, and socially competent citizens. This development is accomplished through a structured program of physical activities. The physical education program should be structured to permit maximum benefits to accrue to the largest possible number of students.

This program also provides a wide variety of physical education experiences in a progressive sequence to meet the youngsters' needs and to challenge their abilities and capacities.

NEEDS OF HIGH SCHOOL STUDENTS

A modern physical education program should be based on certain guiding principles. The key to the design of these principles is found in the formulation of curriculum that recognizes the needs of students. The following physiological, psychological, and sociological principles are designed to meet these overall needs.

Physiological Principles

1. The physical education program should provide ample opportunities for a wide range of movements involving the large muscles.
2. The facts related to the growth and development of children should guide in curriculum construction.
3. Provision should be made in the program for the differences in physical capacities and abilities which are found among students.
4. The physical fitness needs of students must be met by the physical education program.

Psychological Principles

1. The physical education program should consist predominantly of natural play activities.
2. The activities should be selected in the light of the psychological age characteristics of the child as well as the physiological.
3. Activities which are valuable in arousing and expressing emotions should be chosen.
4. In the selection of activities, some provision should be made for progression.
5. In the selection and placement of activities sufficient time should be provided so that the skills may be learned reasonably well.
6. Select activities which best meet the seasonal drives of the students.

Sociological Principles

1. The curriculum should be rich in activities adaptable to use in leisure time.

2. Activities should be selected for their possible contributions to the youth's training for citizenship in a democracy.
3. The curriculum should be suited to the ideals of the community as well as its needs.
4. Activities which are particularly rich in possibilities for individual character training are especially desirable.
5. Activities which reflect the present social order and anticipate future trends should be provided in the program.
6. All students should be taught activities which can be used at home and in the immediate vicinity of the home.

In developing a physical education program which encompasses preceding principles, the following physiological and psychological nature of the senior high school student must be recognized:

Physiological Nature of the High School Student

1. Height and weight–girls comparatively constant, boys rapid rate of growth
2. Strength–girls reach peak at age of sixteen, boys increased greatly
3. Coordination–gradual improvement
4. Skeleton–well calcified; posture poor
5. Circulatory system–age 16–82% of adult efficiency
age 17–90% of adult efficiency
age 18–98.5% of adult efficiency
6. Endurance–better than any previous age
7. Reaction time–better than any previous age
8. Motor ability–increases; eager to perfect skills

Psychological Nature of the High School Student

1. Narrowing of interests; toward specialization
2. Age of loyalty and cooperation; team games
3. Marked development of self-confidence
4. Greater powers of attention and reasoning
5. Strong interest in personal appearance by both sexes
6. Hero worship still a strong influence
7. Fighting tendency is strong in boys; competitive
8. Girls attracted by passive social activities
9. Strong interest in opposite sex
10. Increased interest and ability in leading

The following program was recently adapted at Midpark Senior High School of the Berea City School District. Mr. Neal Hesche, Supervisor of Health and Physical Education for the Berea City Schools, and Mr. Richard Lowry, chairman of the Health and Physical Education Department at Midpark Senior High School, are largely responsible for the development and success of this program.

SENIOR HIGH SCHOOL PHYSICAL EDUCATION PROGRAM

Terminology

The chart which follows indicates the scope of the high school physical education curriculum. The following explanations of terms are offered to enable a clear interpretation of the curriculum.

1. *Content areas:* Physical education at Midpark High School is divided into the following large content areas:

   Team Sports
   Individual and Dual Sports
   Tumbling and Gymnastics
   Acquatics
   Dance and Basic Movements (Girls)
   Physical Fitness
   Electives

2. *Subject areas:* Subject areas are sub-divisions of the content areas; e.g., touch football is a sub-division of the content area of Team Sports; wrestling, a subject area of Individual and Dual Sports.

3. *Electives:* Students have an opportunity to elect some subject areas in which they may wish to specialize. In this program, their ability to pass the required courses in swimming and tumbling and gymnastics will determine the number of electives they are able to select.

4. *Requirements:* Requirements are the directed learning experiences in each content area which each student must satisfy in order to pass the course and receive credit. The individual has a choice within each content area as to the subject area he wishes to follow. Requirements for three high school years:

a. One team sport each year. The sport must be a different one each year.
b. One individual sport each year. The sport must be a different one each year.
c. Boys: One satisfactorily passed course in gymnastics and tumbling. Girls: One satisfactorily passed course in gymnastics and tumbling in sophomore year.
d. Two swim units per year until successful completion of swimming criteria. After this no more swim units are required.
e. One unit of physical fitness required of all boys each year.
f. Girls are required two dance units during junior and senior years.
g. Electives with remaining units.

The requirements that must be filled in three years of high school can be fulfilled only by sophomores starting this program.

Since the Physical Education Department is implementing the program for all grade levels, it has set up separate Physical Education Requirements for the coming school year.

5. *Unit Requirements:* The following list shows the unit requirements for each school year. Sophomore boys' and sophomore and junior girls' requirements will remain constant, with the junior and senior boys' and senior girls' requirements being changed within the next two years to conform to the three-year high school program.

UNIT REQUIREMENTS

BOYS	*(Senior Year)* GIRLS
1. One team sport	1. One team sport
2. One individual sport	2. One individual sport
3. One physical fitness	3. One dance
4. Two swimming units for beginning or intermediate	4. Two swimming units for beginning and intermediate
5. One or two electives by advanced swimmers	5. One or two electives by advanced swimmers

(Junior Year)

1. One team sport each year	1. One team sport
2. One individual sport each year	2. One individual sport
3. Two swim units per year (unless advanced class, then only one)	3. One dance
4. One physical fitness	4. Two swim units for beginning and intermediate. One swim unit for advanced.
5. One elective or two by advanced swimmers	5. One or two electives by advanced swimmers.

(Sophomore Year)

1. One team sport each year (different sport)	1. One team sport each year (different sport)
2. One individual sport each year (different sport)	2. One individual sport each year (different sport)
3. One tumbling and gymnastics	3. One dance
4. Two swim units	4. Two swim units
5. One physical fitness each year	5. One elective

Each subject area within the content area has requirements that each student must satisfactorily pass before receiving credit for the activity.

Since the school year is divided into six 6-week periods, there will be six independent grading periods.

If a student does not satisfactorily pass an activity in one specific six-week period, he will not fail the physical education program for the year. In the case of activities that require prerequisites, the beginning and intermediate courses must be satisfactorily passed before advancing to the more difficult activity.

6. *Prerequisite:* Many subject areas require prerequisite skills acquired in another basic subject area; e.g., prerequisite courses for synchronized swimming. These courses are indicated on the curriculum chart with a double asterisk.
7. *Time Blocks:* A time block is six consecutive weeks of physical education classes.

   In the three-year high school program at Midpark High

School, the total number of weeks (108) is divided into six yearly time blocks. By making slight variations, these time blocks can be adjusted to coincide with the grading periods of the school, the opening and closing of school, and/or winter and spring vacations.

A. Implementation

The physical education program for Midpark High School represents a departure from the traditional program by permitting the student alternate choices and vertical learning opportunities. It is a giant stride toward aiding youth to become responsible, perceiving, self-directing, self-educating individuals who are capable of making rational decisions and value judgments.

The adaptation of the sequential physical education program is only partially that proposed by the Educational Research Council of Greater Cleveland.

1. *Regulatory Factors*

   The regulating factors that had to be considered are as follows:

   a. *Space and Facilities:* They will be so organized that group instruction and individual self-directed activity may take place simultaneously.

   b. *Equipment and Supplies:* They are of sufficient quality and quantity. The Physical Education Department has a planned program for the purchase, maintenance, storage, and replacement of equipment which is essential for the proper growth of the program.

   c. *Teacher-student Assignments:* These will take into account knowledge, personal and physical qualities of the teacher. Proper utilization of staff fosters good student-teacher relationships and desirable educational outcomes.

   There will be a ratio of one teaching station to one teacher to one subject area per class period if a student teacher is made available in each program.

   There is a homogeneous grouping of students.

   d. *Time Allotment:* Time allotment will be adequate to permit the attainment of the educational objectives of the program. (See the previous discussion on time allotment.)

2. *Plan*

   Each physical education class will offer as many different subject areas within each content area as our space, facilities, staff, equipment and supplies, and time allotment will permit.

   a. *Subject Areas Offered for Each Six-Week Period:* The following list shows the exact subject areas within the content area offered each six-week period in both the girls and boys sequential physical education program.

	10th Grade		11th Grade	
Six-week period	Girls	Boys	Girls	Boys
I	1. speedball	physical fitness	hockey, field	physical fitness
	2. soccer	touch football	soccer	touch football
	3. track and field	soccer-speedball	tennis	tennis
	4. advanced swim	advanced swim	advanced senior lifesaving	advanced swim
II	1. gymnastics tumbling	gymnastics tumbling	gymnastics tumbling	physical fitness
	2. basketball	basketball	basketball	basketball
	3. track and field	wrestling	track and field	wrestling
	4. beginning swim	intermediate swim	beginning swim	intermediate swim
III	1. gymnastics tumbling	physical fitness	gymnastics tumbling	physical fitness
	2. modern dance	gymnastics tumbling	badminton table tennis	handball table tennis
	3. badminton table tennis	badminton	modern dance	badminton
	4. intermediate swim	beginning swim	intermediate swim	intermediate swim
IV	1. gymnastics tumbling	gymnastics tumbling	modern dance	physical fitness

Six-week period	10th Grade Girls	10th Grade Boys	11th Grade Girls	11th Grade Boys
	2. volleyball	volleyball	volleyball	volleyball
	3. badminton table tennis	wrestling	golf	badminton
	4. beginning swim	advanced swim	beginning swim	intermediate tumbling gymnastics
V	1. basic movement	physical fitness	basic movement	physical fitness
	2. volleyball	volleyball	volleyball	track and field
	3. folk dance	track and field	modern dance	golf
	4. advanced swim	intermediate swim	advanced swim senior lifesaving	intermediate swim
VI	1. tumbling gymnastics	tumbling gymnastics	tennis	track and field
	2. softball	softball	softball	softball
	3. archery	track and field	track and field	archery
	4. intermediate swim	beginning swim	intermediate swim	beginning swim

b. *Friday Activities:* The following plan of activities will be followed on Fridays during inclement weather conditions if insufficient teaching stations exist to carry on the regular program. Since the facilities will have to be shared, some of the activities are co-educational. By use of the large gymnasium divider, the activities indicated by an asterisk will be carried on separately.

September	Organization Boy's recreational swim Girls have gymnasium physical fitness*
October	Physical fitness*
End of First Six-Week Period	
	Square dance

November	Square dance
December	Square dance
End of Second Six-Week	
	Folk dance Christmas vacation
January	Folk dance Movie on Skiing for all Girls have a movie Boys have gymnasium
End of Third Six-Week Period	
February	Relays* Physical fitness* Boys' recreational swim Girls have gymnasium
March	Girls' recreational swim Boys have gymnasium Girls have a movie Boys have gymnasium
End of Fourth Six-Week Period	
April	Social dance Volleyball* Movie on Water Safety for all
End of Fifth Six-Week Period	
May	Physical fitness*
June	Collect locks

c. *Evaluative Instruments:* The following evaluative instruments will be utilized in the sequential program:
   1. Physical and medical examinations and health appraisals
   2. Strength tests and appraisals
   3. Observation, informal and systematic
   4. Test of activity skills
   5. Teacher-constructed tests
   6. Marks and grading

DEVELOPMENT OF A SECONDARY SCHOOL INTRAMURAL PROGRAM

Successful intramural programs, like any other, must be well organized and properly supervised. Most men, who are willing to devote after school hours, are primarily interested in the interscholastic sports. This frequently limits the field of well qualified intramural directors.

In order to get the maximum in participation, it is highly recommended that the intramural director and the physical education department chairman work closely together on this program. This is especially important when the intramural director is a classroom teacher and has contact with a limited number of students during the day.

DUTIES OF THE INTRAMURAL DIRECTORS

1. To supervise and administer the intramural program for that particular building.
2. To schedule all of the various activities for the intramural program for the school year.
3. To publicize all scheduled events and announce results of various activities.
4. To arrange for the use of the facilities needed for the various activities in the program.
5. To maintain an accurate file of insurance forms for students participating in the program.
6. To submit budgets through the Physical Education Department for items of that school's intramural program.
7. To prepare monthly reports giving a brief synopsis of the activity for that particular time. These reports are sent to the Director of Athletics for inclusion in his report to the Board of Education.
8. To submit an annual report covering the entire school year's activities for this program. These will be included in the Annual Athletic Report.
9. To work closely with the Assistant Intramural Director and to assign his duties and responsibilities.

The intramural insurance form in Figure 6-1 may prove quite helpful.

INTRAMURAL INSURANCE FORM QUESTIONNAIRE

Name ______________________ Grade ______________
Homeroom __________ Section __________ Telephone ______________
Address ______________________ Birthdate ______________

. . . .

Insurance type:

Name of Company ______________
Policy No. __________ Type ______

If the student is not covered by insurance for medical benefits, the school, the intramural department, or the intramural staff will not be responsible for medical fees received as a result of intramural event.

. . . .

Check one:

If your son or daughter is injured during an intramural event, would you:

1. Want him or her taken to the hospital first and then notify the parents, or;
2. Notify the parents to take their son or daughter to the hospital, or;
3. Other (specify)

In case the parents cannot be located, please give the name of a relative or friend:

Name ______________________
Address ______________________
Phone ______________________

Thank you for your cooperation.

Parent's Signature ______________ The Berea City Schools Intramural Departments

Date ______________

Figure 6-1

ELIGIBILITY STANDARDS

All students are eligible to participate in the program with the following exceptions:

1. A student who earns a varsity award in a sport is ineligible to participate in that activity or similar activity (baseball-softball).
2. A student who earns a varsity award at another school in a sport is ineligible to participate in that activity or similar activity (baseball-softball).
3. A student may not participate on more than one team in any activity.
4. A student may not quit a team to join another team once play has begun in that activity.
5. A student who is excused from physical education for physical reasons may not participate unless this participation is approved by the Physical Education Department and the student's family doctor if this is deemed necessary.
6. A student who is a disciplinary problem may be denied participation privileges.

GENERAL PROCEDURES

1. Competition will be open to all students either as individuals, homeroom teams, or as independent teams.
2. Competition will be held after school hours with the exception of those activities which lend themselves better to the mid-day or pre-school recreation periods.
3. All competition will consist of at least one round of play and a minimum of a double elimination.
4. Any competition played with an ineligible player will be considered a forfeit for the team engaging the ineligible player.

AWARDS

1. Certificates to all participants in any phase of the program.
2. Award to champion and runner-up positions in individual competition and table tennis doubles.
3. Award to all members of championship teams.

SPORTS ACTIVITIES

The actual schedule of sports activities will vary greatly; much depends on available facilities, general interest in certain sports, weather conditions, etc. If any degree of interest is shown, that particular activity should be included in the program.

Some of the more popular sports by season are:

Fall

Touch Football
Speedball
Tennis
Field Hockey
Soccer
Archery

Winter

Table Tennis
Basketball
Gymnastics
Swimming

Spring

Volleyball
Track and Field
Softball
Tennis
Golf

One of the biggest mistakes made by most school systems is in planning the use of the gymnasiums. In so many instances very few intramural and athletic activities are scheduled in the gymnasiums during the fall and spring. Then during the winter months not enough time is available for all of the activities that are planned.

This can be remedied by a little imagination and ingenuity on the part of boys and girls intramural directors.

GIRLS ATHLETIC ASSOCIATION

The Girls Athletic Association in most junior and senior high schools is an excellent organization for athletic participation and for social functions.

The aims and objectives of this association shall be:

1. To promote the participation of all girls in a wholesome and diversified program of sports and games.
2. To promote within the individual the development of those qualities which make for good citizenship and sportsmanship.
3. To promote the development of a feeling of friendliness and cooperation through social contacts.
4. To develop an interest and desire for play that will continue in later life.
5. To develop student conducted activities thus encouraging leadership.
6. To aid and promote the development of school spirit and loyalty in all school athletics.

In addition to participation in many sports activities, girls may also serve in such capacities as:

1. Officers
2. Committee chairmen
3. Team managers
4. Photographers
5. Scorekeepers and timers
6. Captains
7. Officials
8. Publicity chairmen
9. Equipment managers

Some of the more popular social events are dances, seasonal parties (Halloween and Christmas), swimming, bowling and skating parties, and invitational playdays.

Playdays involving other schools can be the highlight of the year for both girls and boys intramural programs.

COOPERATION BETWEEN THE INTERSCHOLASTIC, PHYSICAL EDUCATION, AND INTRAMURAL PROGRAMS

Since the interscholastic, physical education, and intramural programs are all important, a continuous effort must be made to insure the promotion and success of each. This involves proper budgeting, use of facilities, and sharing equipment.

Each person involved in the program should be willing to

cooperate with the other departments. They must help promote each others' activities as well as their own.

Periodic meetings involving common problems are important. Helping others to solve these problems is even more vital.

No one phase of the program can ever really move ahead by curtailing another part.

ASSIGNMENT OF PERSONNEL

The proper assignment of personnel is very significant. Several different aspects should be considered.

1. Elementary physical education teachers are frequently interested in coaching. They are often needed, hired, and assigned to a secondary school even though their teaching assignment is in another building. This can present problems since there is little communication between this coach and the principal and students during the school day. If elementary physical education teachers are coaching it is best to employ them as assistants. Since some elementary schools conduct after school programs of their own, this teacher may be needed to supervise these activities. In such cases, he should coach only one sport.
2. In the secondary schools, especially the senior high buildings, the physical education department chairman should assist or direct the intramural program. Because of his contact with so many students in his department and because of his training and background, he can render a real service. He can make certain equipment readily available and usually help in determining the real needs and interests of the students in the intramural program.
3. Physical education department chairmen should not be assigned duties of ticket managers or faculty managers. These activities should be handled by the athletic department.
4. No person should be given more than two assignments. This allows some free time during the year. Involvement in different phases of the program can help them to appreciate the problems in other activities as well as their own.

SEVEN

Procurement and Maintenance of Athletic Equipment and Facilities

Few athletic directors and coaches take the time and effort to familiarize themselves properly with newer trends in equipment and facilities. Yet this is the one area which demands a considerable amount of the total athletic budget.

Most companies and suppliers are very anxious to make pertinent literature available for members of school athletic departments. Recent publications and materials should be obtained, circulated, and read by all staff members.

A thorough knowledge of the proper care and maintenance of equipment and facilities is equally important. The life expectancy of such items can be greatly enhanced and considerable money can be saved.

BASIC PRINCIPLES

The following basic principles should be carefully followed in procurement and maintenance of equipment and facilities.

1) A definite policy for purchasing equipment should be followed. The proper forms should be used and signed by authorized personnel only.

2) All suppliers must be made aware of these purchasing procedures and should be required to comply.
3) Reconditioning and cleaning of equipment should follow athletic department policies. Only authorized companies should be used.
4) Cleaning and reconditioning items must be included in the athletic budget.
5) Schedules for the use and sharing of equipment and facilities must be carefully prepared.
6) Safety factors should be carefully considered at all times in both equipment and facilities.
7) Close cooperation with maintenance and custodial personnel should be established. A carefully planned program for the repairing and maintenance of facilities is vital.
8) Strive for the maximum use and benefit of available equipment and facilities.

SPECIFIC GUIDELINES

The following guidelines may prove helpful in making plans to purchase athletic equipment:

1) Purchase the necessary equipment as it would pertain to inventory of equipment already on hand.
2) Work closely with other sports in major purchases so that the athletic budget is not overloaded with similar requests during the same year.
3) Purchase high grade equipment. This is especially important in materials where safety features are essential.
4) Be certain that equipment meets the necessary standards and dimensions for that particular sport or event.
5) Give the suppliers sufficient time for delivery by purchasing as early as possible. Budgets should be prepared to make this policy possible.
6) Purchase equipment from reliable companies. This is most important in handling problems such as wrong shipments, improper billing, damaged material, etc.
7) Use bid buying procedures if this can be done. If not, make every effort to get the best prices available. Sometimes advantage can be taken of close-out sales and discounts during certain seasons.

8) Select sizes needed based on the present inventory of equipment. Proper fitting of athletes is especially significant in safety and protective gear.

BID BUYING PROCEDURES

There are definite advantages in bid buying if proper care is taken in the description and specifications for each item.

The form shown in Figure 7-1 is used by the Parma City Schools in Parma, Ohio. Each head coach uses this form in requesting the purchase of certain items.

After the budget forms are submitted to the director of athletics, specifications and bid sheets are prepared compiling those items requested.

Figure 7-2 reflects such a compilation.

The notice to bidders, instructions to bidders, and form of proposal shown in Figures 7-3, 7-4, and 7-5 should precede the specification and bid sheets.

The Berea City Schools in Berea, Ohio use the athletic inventory record shown in Figure 7-6. These are prepared by the head coach in each sport at the conclusion of the season. It can be most helpful in accountability of equipment and for the purchase of new material.

Cleaning and Reconditioning

Since most schools are not large enough to own and operate their own laundry, it becomes necessary to use commercial cleaners for this purpose. Some schools will send football game jerseys, pants, and socks home with the players to be laundered by the mothers. This can save the athletic department money, but may also result in improper care, shrinkage, fading, and similar problems.

Most new and expensive game equipment should be sent to professional cleaners. If school laundries are available and used, only properly trained employees should be permitted to operate this equipment.

The cleaning of inflated balls and mats is also an important part of this program. Wrestling mats in particular should be regularly cleaned and disinfected.

Proper reconditioning of athletic equipment can be one of the most expensive items in the budget. This is especially true of

ATHLETIC BUDGET FORM

For School Year 19___-19___

School______________________________
Sport______________________________
Coach______________________________

	Normandy	Parma	Valley Forge	Greenbriar	Hillside	Pleasant Valley	Schaaf	Shiloh			Description of item, brand name & model no., color, design, sizes and quantity	Unit Price	TOTAL
									DEPT.	TOTAL			

SPECIFICATIONS AND BID SHEETS FOR
PHYSICAL EDUCATION, BASEBALL, GOLF, TRACK AND TENNIS

PHYSICAL EDUCATION

Line	*Quantity*	*Description of Item*	*Brand Name & Model No. Bid on*	*Unit*	*TOTAL*
		(Acceptable brand name and model numbers listed. Bidder is to state brand name and model number on which his bid is based.)			
1	3 gr.	*Tennis Balls,* Wilson T 1020			
2	10 dz.	*Practice golf balls,* Uniroyal Range Super V construction with stripe (red)			
3	1	*Cata-pole* Model No. A1440, 14 feet-140#, Pacer American			
4	1	*Cata-pole* Model No. 1550-15 feet, 150#, Pacer American			
5	1	*Track timer,* 3 separate dials (minutes, seconds and tenth of seconds) Jungham Three Face Timer, Wolverine No. M			
6	2	*Split Timer,* Hanhart No. 786/-A/10, Wolverine No. H-13			
7	4	*Discus, rubber,* official high school, Gill #307			
8	4	*Indoor Shot, 12#*–Gill #341			
9	1	*Outdoor Shot, 12#*–Gill #331			
10	1	*Outdoor Shot, 16#*–Gill #332			

Figure 7-2

PARMA BOARD OF EDUCATION
6726 Ridge Road
Parma, Ohio 44129

NOTICE TO BIDDERS

Sealed bids will be received by the Clerk-Treasurer of the Parma City School District, 6726 Ridge Road, Parma 44129, Cuyahoga County, Ohio until twelve o'clock noon, Eastern Standard Time on

DATE DESIRED

for furnishing Physical Education, Baseball, Golf, Track and Tennis supplies listed and described in these specifications for the Athletic and Physical Education Department.

Figure 7-3

INSTRUCTIONS TO BIDDERS

1. *Proposals*

Each proposal shall be filled out on the accompanying bidding form, giving complete and detailed prices required in this contract. No oral, telephone or telegraphic proposals will be considered. All proposals must be signed by the bidder, giving business address. In the case of firms or corporations, proposals must be signed by the authorized officers. Proposals must be in sealed envelopes and plainly marked, "BIDS ON PHYSICAL EDUCATION, BASKETBALL, GOLF, TRACK AND TENNIS."

2. *Delivery*

Prices shall include delivery. Delivery destination will be the Parma Board of Education, 6726 Ridge Road, Parma, Ohio 44129. No deliveries on Saturday, Sunday, holidays, or after 4:00 P.M. on any day.

3. *Sales and Excise Tax Exemptions*

All contractors shall note that

(a) The Owner is exempt from the Ohio Retail Sales Tax.

(b) The Owner is exempt from the Federal Manufacturers' Excise Tax. Refund of this tax, where paid, can be obtained by the manufacturer by filing Form No. 843 of the Department of Internal Revenue.

(c) The Owner is exempt from the Federal Transportation Tax where he is consignee of the material shipped.

(d) There is, of course, the usual exemption from the Ohio Gasoline Excise Tax, where the fuel is consumed in stationary gas engines or in equipment which does not operate on public highways.

The contractor may or may not take these items into consideration in submitting his bid. The Owner assumes no responsibility whatever as to which items are Sales tax exempt and which are not so exempt.

Figure 7-4

PARMA CITY SCHOOL DISTRICT
6726 Ridge Road
Parma, Ohio 44129

FORM OF PROPOSAL

PROJECT: Physical Education, Baseball, Golf, Track and Tennis Supplies

BIDS DUE: Date desired–12:00 Noon
Eastern Standard Time

DELIVER BIDS TO: The Board of Education
Parma City School District
6726 Ridge Road
Parma, Ohio 44129

ATTENTION: Mr. Harry Gerwin
Purchasing Agent

Signed: ______________________________
Company ______________________________
Address ______________________________
____
Delivery Date ______________________________
Phone Number ____________________ Area Code ____________

Date ____________________

Figure 7-5

BEREA CITY SCHOOLS

Athletic Inventory Record

NAME OF SPORT________________ DATE____________

COACH____________________

Quantity	Description	Size	New	*Condition* Excellent	Good	Fair	Poor	Discard

Figure 7-6

football equipment. Some schools will attempt to sterilize and recondition equipment by using their own coaches and equipment managers after the regular season is completed. This may be done rather satisfactorily with some equipment. However, any protective equipment, such as football helmets and shoulder pads, should be handled by professional reconditioners. Too much is at stake to cut corners when it may impair the safety of any of the athletes.

The proper storage of equipment during the off-season is most important. by using areas that are dry, cool, and well ventilated, the life of equipment will be greatly lengthened. Athletic directors and coaches should frequently inspect these storage areas as a safeguard against insects, moisture, and possible theft.

FACILITIES CONSTRUCTION

Several books have been written dealing primarily with the construction and maintenance of facilities. It would be impossible to do justice to this topic in a portion of a chapter.

The director of athletics should, however, have an important part in helping to plan new facilities and in the maintenance of these facilities. He should work closely with the architects and provide pertinent information and suggestions for constructing these facilities.

Much information is available as to dimensions of courts, fields, and other play areas, and therefore will not be included here.

The director of athletics should be familiar with the newest trends, types of construction, and the latest maintenance procedures. He should be kept informed by the board of education and the superintendent of schools as to student enrollment figures, plans for future construction, community involvement in use of facilities, etc.

The following information was made available to the architects by Mr. Rex Smith, Director of Athletics of the Parma City Schools in Parma, Ohio, when Valley Forge Senior High School was being planned. This school has an enrollment of 2800 students (grades 10-12):

Clinic

The Clinic is to be a part of the Health and Physical Education suite of the new high school. Locate the Clinic adjacent to the Health classroom which is provided for Physical Education instruction. A full time nurse will be in the clinic. The clinic should have an examination room and separate rest areas for boys and girls.

Gymnasium

The gymnasium should contain a playing floor 50 x 84 feet with a minimum of 8' between the end line and the wall. Study the desirability of using a floating floor iron-bound in design. There should be an electric divider door making two units out of the gymnasium. A balcony or balconies might well be used with roll-back bleachers providing extra instruction space. In this space corrective gym, archery, wrestling, tennis, etc., could be taught. Below the balcony could be either corridors or dressing rooms. Most of the seats are to be at the sides. Twenty-five hundred seats should be provided. Plexiglas blisters could be used on the roof, providing better light than can be provided by side windows. The ceiling heights can be kept low in all areas, except the main gymnasium.

Gymnasium Lobby

Make the lobby a part of the corridor or provide for other multi-use. Provide for crowd control so that no check-out is needed when a person goes into the lobby and toilet areas from the gymnasium. Place the ticket booth outside of the control area, and sales area for candy, etc., inside the control area.

Gymnasium Dressing Rooms

BOYS

1. One physical education dressing room for eighty with lockers set up for nine sections.
2. Two varsity rooms of sixty lockers in each. Include area for team meetings and projection.
3. One shower room common to both of the locker rooms. Central control of water with a mixing valve, and one independent shower head on separate control. Make floors of the shower and the drying room area of slip-resistant ceramic tile.
4. One drying room next to shower room.
5. Provide small towel room near shower drying room.

GIRLS

1. Physical education dressing room for eighty with lockers for nine sections.
2. One central shower room—central control of water with mixing valve and three individual shower booths.
3. One drying room next to shower room.
4. Provide small towel room near shower drying room.

Gymnasium Offices

Men—Room for six desks; individual dressing room and shower.

Women—Room for three desks; individual dressing room and shower.

Both should be close to locker room and gymnasium.

Gymnasium Equipment Drying Rooms

Boys—Six small, closet-size, with pull-out racks and power vent to roof. Also heat (off from varsity room).

Gymnasium Training Room

Small—next to Varsity Room; two tables; whirlpool bath; heat lamps; ice pack sink in floor.

Gymnasium Supply Room

Long, high, and narrow, with dispensing window to boys' varsity room. Two equipment rooms open to gymnasium floor.

Swimming Pool

The pool should be an alternate to take off if costs will not allow. The swimming pool is to be simple in design and 45' by 75'1". It should provide seating for four hundred spectators. The pool tank should be finished in white tile. The floors should be ceramic mosaic tile. The ceiling of the room should be of corrugated aluminum acoustic material. Provide portable starting blocks at the end of the swimming pool. The ceiling height of the swimming pool should be high enough to use a one meter board. No viewing window underneath the water or underwater lights will be needed. Aluminum doors in all entrances to the pool are to be used. There should be no exterior doors from the pool. A nine foot deck on one side of the pool, a twelve foot deck on the other side of the pool, a ten foot deck at the end of the pool, and a fifteen foot deck at the end of the diving board will be sufficient.

Laundry Room

A laundry area is to be included that will contain a washer, extractor, and dryer. It will be used to launder the towels, tank suits, and some of the athletic equipment. A towel fee will be charged so that the cost will be covered by the students. Approximately 1,000 towels per day will be washed. During the peak athletic season an additional four hundred will be processed.

MAINTENANCE PROGRAM

The proper maintenance of athletic facilities is one of the major problems confronting athletic directors today. Such care and upkeep require considerable planning, equipment to do the work, and cooperation with the maintenance department in the school system. This program also needs the support of building principals, coaches, and the student body to be really successful.

Periodic meetings with the buildings and grounds supervisor, the business manager, and the director of athletics should be planned. Common problems relating to the staff, equipment, facilities, financial aspects, work schedule, new construction, and general philosophy need attention. Much can be accomplished through meetings of this type which will benefit both the athletic department and the maintenance department in achieving a common goal.

The director of athletics should be consulted when buying materials and equipment that pertain to the athletic facilities. Care should be taken to observe safety precautions and to abide by the rules and regulations of the state athletic associations regarding the use of materials and equipment.

The sharing of brochures and other pertinent literature by the athletic department and the maintenance department can be of mutual benefit.

The buildings and grounds supervisor or other person responsible for establishing standards for the operation of the maintenance department must protect the facilities by purchasing quality products. The money saved by selecting inferior and less expensive items can eventually cost the schools more money. Proper planning and record keeping can reflect true savings in this regard.

Since most custodians are not experts in gymnasium floor maintenance, the buildings and grounds supervisor should have workshops headed by representatives of leading floor refinishing companies. Such problems as floor buckling, treating worn or thin spots and marred or darkened areas, stripping the floor, etc. are important.

Some aspects of this work, such as sanding, usually require professional care.

CARE AND MAINTENANCE OF ARTIFICIAL TURF

Artificial turf is relatively new and improvements are constantly being made. Despite this progress, care and maintenance is necessary to get the maximum in usage and value.

The Recreation and Athletic Products, 3 M Co. of St. Paul, Minnesota, has prepared an excellent booklet for care and maintenance of artificial turf from this material. Cleaning can be divided into these areas:

1) Litter Removal

Litter, such as peanut shells, paper, sunflower seeds, etc., can best be removed by using one of the many lawn sweepers or lawn vacuums available at all lawn and garden shops. Models are available from 25 inch push sweepers to 30 inch self-propelled units. Selection of number, size, and type of units should be based upon available manpower and time allotted to clean the individual field.

2) Dirt Removal

To prevent dirt and soil from becoming imbedded deep into the Turf, vacuum clean with an industrial type carpet vacuum which utilizes a beater bar or brush regularly. This will help prolong the life of the Turf and may eliminate the need for eventual detergent scrubbing.

3) Dirt Removal–Shampooing

Regular vacuum cleaning is by far the preferred method for cleaning the field. However, in the event that regular vacuum cleaning is not performed or is not satisfactory because of peculiar local conditions, a shampooing procedure is recommended. Local conditions that would warrant shampooing include sooty atmospheric pollution and any condition leading to buildup of oily residue.

4) Stain Removal

For removal of stains on the field from an unknown source, try these three steps first: (1) Brush the stain with a stiff fiber brush; (2) Scrub the area with soap and water; (3) Flush with lots of clear water and dry area with a towel. If this fails to remove the stain, apply a dry cleaning solution such as Renuzit or trichlorethylene to the stained area with a damp cloth. For stains of a known source, apply the procedure in Figure 7-7.

5) Snow Removal

When snow is expected prior to a game you should cover your turf with a tarpaulin. Light snows may then be brushed off of the tarpaulin and the tarpaulin removed in the conventional manner just as with a grass field. Heavy snows, of course, would have to be removed with a snow plow or snow blower before the tarpaulin could be removed. Avoid the use of chains or metal cleats on the tires of the snow plow; also avoid spinning the wheels of snow plows as this could possibly generate enough heat to fuse the fibers together and damage the turf.

Extra precautions should be taken to avoid cuts in the turf by snow plow blades or other equipment. A rubber tip on the snow plow blade is a necessity. If no tarp is used, or if snow occurs during a game, the field can be cleared with a plow equipped with a rubber tipped blade. Excess snow then can be removed by sweeping; a bamboo "turf" brush is available for such sweeping.

6) Removal of Water

All synthetic turf fields are constructed in order to provide for water drainage. There are many instances when this drainage is not adequate.

Excessive moisture may be removed by equipment which squeezes water from the turf and picks it up. It consists of an engine, pumps, rollers, nozzles, and a water tank.

TYPE OF STAIN	REMOVAL METHOD
1. *Water Soluble* Alcohol Fruit-juice Soft drinks Urine Washable ink	1. Scrub area with a solution of warm water and detergent. Rinse thoroughly to remove all traces of soap. Dry with absorbent towels.
2. *Oily* Ball point pen ink Grease Vehicle grease Oil	2. Sponge area with a dry cleaning solvent such as Renuzit or Trichlorethylene.
3. *Water Soluble and Oily* Blood Chocolate Coffee Egg Ice cream Milk Shoe Polish Vomit Tobacco juice	3. Sponge area with a detergent solution, followed by Trichlorethylene or Renuzit, if necessary.
4. *Heavy Grease and Grime* Candle wax Chewing gum Crayon Heavy grease Lipstick Tar	4. Wax and gum: Wrap ice cube in a clean cloth and hold against substance until hardened, then remove. Sponge area with dry cleaning solution if a stain remains. For remainder of list, use dry cleaning solvent, then detergent. Rinse with clear water.

Figure 7-7

EIGHT

Developing Relevant Eligibility Procedures for Athletes

The role of properly administering sound eligibility procedures for senior and junior high schools is most significant. Oftentimes principals and athletic directors may tend to minimize the importance of this phase of the athletic program.

Little is said when the eligibility procedures are correctly and efficiently functioning. On the other hand, few matters can cause worse publicity than an error in preparing eligibility certificates or in allowing ineligible students to participate.

Much of the constitution and rules of the different state athletic associations is based on the effect that they will have on the eligibility of the athletes involved. More frequently than not, it is the student who is declared ineligible and is the one who suffers. Seldom is the principal, coach, athletic director, or school penalized for negligence in these matters.

This chapter attempts to develop relevant procedures in dealing with eligibility matters.

BASIC RESPONSIBILITY

The building principal is directly responsible for eligibility matters in all cases. He may delegate these duties to the director of athletics, guidance counselor or to a competent secretary or clerk. However, he is the one who signs these lists attesting to their accuracy and validity.

The building principal must keep abreast of all new rules and regulations which are now part of the state athletic association's constitution. He must be well versed in the older rules and should constantly review these, so there is no misunderstanding as to their proper interpretation and application.

He should be certain that if other persons are delegated the responsibility of working in eligibility matters they are properly informed as to their exact duties. They must be given access to the rules and regulations of the state athletic association and of the local district of which they are a part.

No one involved in dealing with eligibility assignments of any kind should assume that their interpretation is necessarily correct. Frequent contacts with the state commissioner is most important for proper rulings. Accurate files and correspondence on cases of a questionable matter should also be maintained.

After the eligibility lists are prepared for the approaching season, the building principal should carefully recheck them. This is most important with the fall season, since it involves problems of passing subjects for the previous semester, passing subjects for the year, summer school courses taken, and other similar situations.

Transfers from private schools and from out-of-state schools should be carefully processed. No student should be allowed to participate until all of the proper paperwork has been received and is in order.

The certificates used by the Ohio High School Athletic Association in processing athletic transfers is shown in Figure 8-1.

PROCEDURE IN EACH BUILDING

A uniform policy in dealing with eligibility should be carefully followed in each building. Since the building principal is responsible for this phase of the program, the exact procedures may vary slightly from one school to the next even within the same school district.

It is mandatory, however, to stay within the framework of the respective state athletic association's rules and regulations at all times.

OHIO HIGH SCHOOL ATHLETIC ASSOCIATION

Athletic Transfer Certificate

To Principal..of..High School

City ....State ....

The .... High School must have, in order to determine his eligibility for athletics, the information requested below regarding a former student in your school. This information is in addition to that usually obtained from a Transfer of Credits. An early reply will be appreciated in the stamped addressed envelope enclosed.

Very truly yours,

....High School ....Principal

Date ....Post Office ....Ohio

1. Student's Name.. Record of Birth..
   Mo. Day Year
   Place of Birth..Source of information: School record ☐ Birth Certificate ☐ Student ☐ Parent ☐
2. In what month and year did this student finish 8th grade classification? Month.................... Year....................
3. In what month and year did this student *first enroll* in the 9th grade? Month.................... Year....................
4. Subjects carried his *last semester* in your school with grades and credit value..
5. Has this student to your knowledge, ever participated in any *interscholastic* game in any sport since having completed the sixth grade? (Participation in a game, either as a regular or as a substitute on the varsity, reserve or any other interscholastic team even for only a minute constitutes participation) ....
6. Would this student have been eligible for interscholastic athletics had he remained in your school?....................
   If not, why not?..
7. Do you know of any reason why he should not be considered eligible in our school?....................If so, please explain ....
8. Is there any additional investigation we should make? ....

Signature of Principal of high school from which student transferred

....

Date..

Figure 8-1

The same procedures should be in effect for all sports regardless of the squad sizes or the emphasis that is placed in certain areas.

In Ohio and other states as well, it is necessary to check the eligibility of students on a weekly basis. This will necessitate the distribution of squad lists for each sport during that entire season. These forms will probably be given to the teachers on Monday morning and collected on Tuesday morning at the latest. The work done during the past week may determine the status of the player for the following week. It is most important to get these lists returned by Tuesday so that the coach will not be planning his practices for the next game around a player who is ineligible.

Shown in Figure 8-2 is a weekly eligibility form used at Berea High School in Berea, Ohio. This is given to each teacher for his particular courses. He should record any failures and make suggestions for improving the student's work.

There are other policies that may be used for teachers to check the work of the athletes. Some schools use a card listing the student's name, the subjects he is taking, and a place at the right for the teacher's name and the cummulative grade for that semester. One good feature of this plan is that the athlete must see his teachers personally to get the card checked and signed. It gives the teacher an excellent opportunity to counsel the student and assist him in his work.

This is probably one of the best procedures to follow as far as the student-teacher relationship is concerned. One problem lies in collecting the cards from the students, and in making certain that all of his teachers have been contacted. The other criticism comes from the teachers themselves. They often feel that this process is too much work and too time consuming.

Other schools use a check list approach where the eligibility sheets are posted on the teacher's bulletin board. The teacher in turn checks the lists and records failing or below standard work on the part of the athletes. This policy requires no effort on the part of the student. Unfortunately it may not require much more effort on the part of the teacher.

It is the easiest plan in many ways to administer, but is quite conducive to a haphazard attitude in dealing with eligibility matters.

A definite policy is necessary in making athletes' records available to college coaches who are recruiting. The building

BEREA HIGH SCHOOL TEACHERS' NAME________________

ATHLETIC ELIGIBILITY

Weekly information needed for participants in________________________
Sport

(*Note:* This sheet will be returned to you each week. Please mark it carefully)

DATES BY WEEK

Name									Subject

Figure 8-2

principal owes allegiance to his students and coaches alike, and must be certain that he enforces a set procedure in such matters.

COMMUNICATION WITH TEACHERS

As efficient and well organized as many principals and athletic directors are today, they too frequently fail to provide the teachers with the necessary information needed in dealing with eligibility matters. Even the better, more experienced teachers have little working knowledge in this area.

What can we do then to better communicate with the staff in making more clear the importance of sound eligibility procedures? The following list may prove helpful.

1. Distribute information sheets to the staff on pertinent items that pertain to them as teachers.
2. Don't burden the teachers with confusing rules and cases that may tend to make their role more difficult.
3. Include on the agenda at teachers' meetings at least twice a year. The beginning of each semester is the best time.
4. Explain to the students how they are being graded. They should also be encouraged to work with the students to improve their marks.
5. The importance of carefully checking the eligibility lists must be stressed.
6. Teachers must be certain not to lower grades to render a student ineligible because he may be a discipline problem. These matters should be refined to the principal, who may declare the student ineligible for discipline reasons.
7. The entire staff should be encouraged to work hard to keep students eligible. The students must also be encouraged to work to their capacity.

ROLE OF THE ATHLETIC DIRECTOR

The part that the director of athletics must play in assisting with eligibility procedures is most significant. He must work very closely with the principal, coaches, and teachers in helping to make decisions in cases which pertain to schools outside of the system. He must also cooperate in setting policies which only affect schools within the system. The director of athletics should make certain that he is well versed in the rules and regulations of the state athletic association. He must also be familiar with the constitution of the conference to which his school belongs. This is very important since eligibility problems may result from violations of these rules.

In some schools the principal gives complete authority to the director of athletics to administer the eligibility program. This trend is becoming more common as the duties of building principals increase.

The thinking on this policy can also work in reverse. Since the director of athletics is extremely busy with many responsibilities of his own, the principal should supervise all of the eligibility matters.

In the opinion of many athletic administrators, this is the one area in interscholastic sports that is still the building principal's responsibility. This is understandable since the academic achievements of the athlete is the basis for determining his eligibility.

The director of athletics should work closely with the state athletic association in establishing new and better eligibility procedures for its member schools. A recent example in Ohio helps illustrate this point:

The Ohio High School Athletic Directors Association has recommended to the state board of control of the Ohio High School Athletic Association a procedure which could eliminate the mailing of eligibility certificates to opponents on a weekly basis. The present rule states that "three days before each contest the administrative head of each school shall mail to the other an eligibility certificate that the persons named are eligible under the rules to represent the school in the contest on the date specified. In the case of a joint meet in which two or more schools compete, the certificates shall be mailed to the manager of the meet. Each school should possess the certificate from the other school before the game begins."

This rule would be changed to eliminate the many different mailings to the opposing schools during the week of the game to be played. It would instead require each school to mail eligibility certificates to all schools on their schedule prior to the opening date for that particular season. If there are changes in these lists at the end of the semester or even the week, revised certificates should be mailed to the opposing schools affected.

Such a rule change will enable schools to save much time and many bookkeeping problems in mailing these certificates.

The form shown in Figure 8-3 is used in Ohio by all schools that are members of the Ohio High School Athletic Association. It is to be processed for all interscholastic athletic events and is mailed to the principal or athletic director of the opposing school. Any boy whose name appears on this list is certified to be eligible. In the event of an error on this list or the omission of a name, this may be corrected by telephone prior to the game. A letter should follow to verify in writing what was said on the telephone.

COACHES' COOPERATION

The head coach in every sport must play an important role in working with eligibility procedures. Some coaches are inclined to get too involved while others fail to do their share. These are certain guidelines that every head coach should follow to properly assist with this program.

First, he should supply the principal with an accurate list of the players on his squad. He should be certain that no boys are omitted and that each name is correctly spelled. The omission of names can become a real problem when some boys are allowed to report to the team at a later date than others because of overlapping reasons.

Second, he must be willing to work closely with the teachers in encouraging his team members to achieve to the best of their ability in all of their courses. Some teachers tend to use the coach as a means of administering discipline to athletes they cannot control. Strangely enough they are usually not contacted during the off-season. Coaches may resent this burden, but at the same time can greatly enhance their image and that of the athletic department.

Third, a good coach will maintain close communication with the parents of boys having eligibility problems. The parents are normally very receptive to this approach and are usually glad to cooperate. In so many cases they may be unaware of the poor academic work that their son is doing.

Fourth, he should be willing to meet with the building principal, director of athletics, and the parents of players who have serious eligibility problems. These may entail the loss of competition for a semester or an entire school year, depending on the situation. Since most parents are poorly informed and ill advised on eligibility matters, the importance of such meetings is even greater.

SEND TO OHSAA PRIOR TO FIRST GAME OR MEET

Ohio High School Athletic Association

(To be exchanged by each school at least three days before contest.)

Official Eligibility Certificate

The following players are eligible under the rules of the O. H. S. A. A. to represent the .... High School in the .... game to be played at ...., ... P.M., on .... 19 . Admission is .... cents.

The officials will be ....

PLEASE USE TYPEWRITER

CONTESTANTS' NAMES ARRANGED ALPHABETICALLY LAST NAME FIRST	BIRTH RECORD USE CERTIFIED BIRTH CERTIFICATE		SCHOOL ATTENDED LAST SEMESTER	DATE OF ENROLLMENT THIS SEMESTER	NUMBER SEMESTERS ENROLLED GRADES 9-12 INCLUDING PRESENT SEMESTER	NUMBER UNITS OF CREDIT PASSED LAST SEMESTER
	MONTH, DAY, YEAR	COUNTY AND STATE				
Davis, Harry	Aug. 15, 1951	Franklin, Ohio	Central H. S.	Sept. 5	5	1.5

Figure 8-3

Fifth, the coach should be very knowledgeable on rules in his sport that may jeopardize a player's eligibility. This cannot be overemphasized. He should clearly spell out exactly what the players can and cannot do before, during, and after the season. This may pertain to such matters as attending summer camps, playing on independent teams during and after the season, receiving certain awards that could render him a professional, etc.

Sixth, he must be willing to comply with the rules of the state athletic association and those of his school district. Occasionally a coach may even desire to have the standards for his particular sport more rigid than those of the other sports. This may create problems within the coaching staff and among the other faculty members as well. In certain cases coaches may tend to deviate from these requirements if they are still within the framework of the state and local rules. This is not only an inconsistency but may reflect favoritism toward the better athletes on the team.

STATUS OF THE INELIGIBLE PLAYER

The question of what to do in regard to the ineligible player is one that every director of athletics must resolve. The status of these athletes may vary from one week to an entire school year. Each school district may have a somewhat different policy but at least they should have one in writing.

1. An ineligible player may practice with the varsity, junior varsity or junior high school teams.
2. He must have a parent permission card signed and on file in the principal's office.
3. He must also have a physical examination form signed by a physician and on file in the principal's office.
4. He must be properly covered by the approved insurance program of the school.
5. He may not participate in any team game at any level.
6. If the principal or coach feels that an athlete should not be practicing with the team because of citizenship attitude or scholastic work, he may be denied the privilege of practicing with the team.

PARTICIPATION FORMS

The card shown in Figure 8-4 is used by the Ohio High School Athletic Association member schools and requires the signature of

....
(Please Print) Last Name First Name Initial School

.........................., 19 .... Date of Birth........................ Place of Birth..
Date

KEEP IN HIGH SCHOOL OFFICE

OHIO HIGH SCHOOL ATHLETIC ASSOCIATION

STUDENT PARTICIPATION, PARENTAL APPROVAL AND PHYSICAL EXAMINATION FORM

This application to participate in interscholastic athletics at the above-named high school is voluntary on my part and is made with the understanding that I have never received any money, or other valuable considerations worth more than one dollar ($1.00), for participation in athletic events, and that I have never competed under an assumed name, after I have represented my high school in any sport. I further agree to abide by the Constitution, Rules, By-laws, Decisions and Interpretations of the Ohio High School Athletic Association.

Signature of Student ______________________________

Parent or Guardian's Permission

I hereby give my consent for the above-named high school student to engage in interscholastic athletics at the above-named high school in the Ohio High School Athletic Association approved sports NOT CIRCLED ON THE OTHER SIDE OF THIS CARD, and to accompany the team as a member on its out-of-town trips. I further consent to treatment of any sort deemed necessary by any physician designated by proper school authorities for any illness or injury resulting from his athletic participation.

Signature of Parent or Guardian ______________________________

Note: This form should be completely filled out and filed in the office of the high school principal, superintendent, or Executive Head of schools prior to student's participation.

Figure 8-4

the athlete's parent or guardian. It grants permission for the athlete to participate on any team during the entire school year. No student may participate until this form is on file in the principal's office.

The form shown in Figure 8-5 is actually the reverse side of the parent permission card used by member schools of the Ohio High School Athletic Association. This side must be properly filled in by the examining physician before the student is allowed to participate. One physical examination is required each school year. However, it is recommended to have athletes reexamined following a serious injury or illness.

MAINTAINING AN AMATEUR STATUS

Since only amateurs are eligible to compete, we must work diligently to protect the athlete from being ruled a professional. Rule 10, Section 1 of the Constitution and Rules of the Ohio High School Athletic Association lists several guidelines, the violation of which could jeopardize a student's amateur status. These may vary somewhat from one state to the next, but are basically alike:

1. Pupils representing member schools must be amateurs.
2. A pupil is ineligible if he receives or is promised money or other valuable considerations for competing in a sport recognized by the Ohio High School Athletic Association. This rule applies throughout the twelve months of the year. A professional in one of these sports is a professional in all. A pupil may play with or against those who receive pay without losing.
3. Acceptance of money or other valuable considerations as expenses or merchandise prizes renders a pupil ineligible. No money is to be given to a contestant. However, it is permissible to accept necessary meals, lodging, and transportation while competing. Medals or trophies may be accepted. College scholarships may be accepted but the amount of the scholarship must be paid directly to the college of choice by the donors.
4. A pupil is ineligible if he competes under an assumed name.
5. The purchase of memberships for specific junior or senior high school members of athletic teams, in youth serving

....
(Please Print) Name of Student City and State

PHYSICAL EXAMINATION SUMMARY

(To be filled out and signed by examining physician)

Grade.................... Age.................... Height.................... Weight.................... Blood Pressure....................

Significant Illness or Injuries..

....

....

Examination	Satis.	Unsatis.
Vision		
Hearing		
Cardiovascular		
Respiratory		
Liver, spleen, kidney, hernia, genitalia		
Extremities		

Examination	Satis.	Unsatis.
Orthopedic		
Neurological		
Skin		
Indicated lab. tests		

Comments on Unsatisfactory Conditions..

....

....

I certify that I have on this date examined the above student and recommend him as being physically able to compete in supervised athletic activities NOT CIRCLED BELOW:

BASEBALL	FIELD HOCKEY	GYMNASTICS	SWIMMING	VOLLEYBALL
BASKETBALL	FOOTBALL	SOCCER	TENNIS	*WRESTLING
CROSS COUNTRY	GOLF	SOFTBALL	TRACK	OTHER....................

*Student may be permitted weight loss to make a lower weight class in WRESTLING. Yes.................... ; No....................

If "Yes", may lose .... pounds.

...., 19.......... ....
Date Signature of Examining Physician

Address.. Tel....................

Figure 8-5

agencies, athletic clubs, recreation centers, etc. would be a violation of this rule. This does not infringe on the right of such organizations to provide anonymously sponsored memberships for individuals in the community proven financially in need.

6. The signing of any contract by a pupil whereby he agrees to compete in any athletic competition for profit, makes said pupil ineligible for further interscholastic athletic competition.

Professional baseball and college try-outs which interfere with a high school student's work or which involve a game in violation of the Ohio High School Athletic Association rules may result immediately in that student's ineligibility for further interscholastic athletic competition.

NINE

Building Schedules, Hiring Officials, and Dealing with Transportation

This chapter deals with three very important and common aspects of any interscholastic athletic program. Without the proper administering of these functions, there is really no program at all. These areas will be treated in a practical and realistic manner and can apply to any school system.

AFFILIATION AND RELATIONS WITH OTHER SCHOOLS

Very few high schools attempt to compete in interscholastic athletics without some sort of conference or league affiliation. Those schools that are not presently in a conference are usually looking for one, and those schools that are about to withdraw from a conference invariably have another in mind.

Leagues come and go; changes within existing conferences have re-alignments of schools on an average of once every five years. These changes often result in revising constitutions and by-laws plus an "about-face" in the general thinking of the member schools.

Several criteria are used in determining conference affiliation. The location and size of the schools are the two most common reasons for comprising athletic leagues. Things such as facilities and game attendance are also considered.

A number of other items are later divulged and sometimes prove to be the real problem areas. For example, do the schools in your conference have a common interest in activities other than athletics? If not, try to remedy these differences by competition in debate, intramural play day programs, chorus contests, one act plays, etc.

Second–Is there a common philosophy in the overall program? Does each school attempt to field respectable teams in all sports? If not, a real effort should be made in this respect.

Third–Is there complete cooperation in the enforcement of rules and regulations by all member schools? There is no valid excuse for doing otherwise.

Fourth–Is there proper treatment shown to the visiting schools in all sports? Are all existing facilities well maintained and clean? Any school that is not a good host is not a good member school.

Nearly all athletic leagues and conferences operate within the framework of a constitution. These should be reviewed periodically and up-dated whenever necessary.

The constitution of the Greater Cleveland Conference is shown in Figure 9-1. This league consists of eight senior high schools with enrollments of 1500 to 2400 in the three grades.

CONSTITUTION
OF
THE GREATER CLEVELEND CONFERENCE

ARTICLE I
NAME

Sec. 1 The name of this conference shall be:
"THE GREATER CLEVELAND C ONFERENCE."

ARTICLE II
MEMBERSHIP

Sec. 1 Application for membership to this conference shall be made in writing filed with the Executive Secretary-Treasurer.

Figure 9-1

Sec. 2 Election to membership shall be by a unanimous affirmative vote of the total membership in this conference at time membership application is received.

Sec. 3 Any school desiring to withdraw from membership in this conference shall present a written request to the Executive Secretary-Treasurer two years prior to its desired date of withdrawal.

ARTICLE III
OFFICERS

Sec. 1 Officers of this Conference shall consist of a president, a vice-president, and the executive secretary-treasurer.

Sec. 2 The president and the vice-president shall be named at the first semester business meeting of each school year. Each shall serve until replaced the following school year.

Sec. 3 Rotation of offices of president and vice-president shall be as follows: Bedford, Maple Heights, Berea, Mayfield, Mentor, Midpark, Willoughby South, Eastlake North.

Sec. 4 The executive secretary-treasurer shall be appointed by a majority vote of the membership of this conference.

ARTICLE V
MEETINGS

Sec. 1 One dinner meeting (early fall semester) each year for administrative and coaching staffs of all conference schools.

Sec. 2 One regular business meeting of this conference shall be held each semester of each school year–first semester in October; second semester in February.

Sec. 3 Official representation of each school shall be limited to principal and athletic director.

Sec. 4 A quorum shall consist of two-thirds of the membership.

Sec. 5 President has authority to call special meetings as needed.

ARTICLE VI
SCHEDULES

Sec. 1 Recognized conference schedules shall be maintained in the following sports: Baseball, Basketball, Cross Country, Football, Golf, Track, Wrestling, Tennis, and Swimming.

Sec. 2 Schedules in other sports may be added by a two-thirds affirmative vote of the membership.

Figure 9-1 *(con't.)*

Sec. 3 A conference sport must be one in which five or more schools enter teams.

ARTICLE VII
OFFICIALS

Sec. 1 Officials for conference contests shall be appointed by the executive secretary-treasurer in basketball, football, and wrestling.

Sec. 2 Officials for conference contests in baseball, cross country, golf, and track shall be obtained by home school with approval of visiting school.

Sec. 3 There shall be *four* paid officials at all conference varsity football contests; *three* paid officials at all junior varsity football games (effective in 1969 season); *three* paid officials at all basketball contests (third official to be used in junior varsity game only, with varsity officials each working one half of varsity game); *two* paid umpires at all baseball games; *two* paid officials at all wrestling contests (one for varsity and one for junior varsity); *one* paid official at all track meets.

ARTICLE VIII
TROPHIES

Sec. 1 Trophies shall be provided by the conference for the championship schools in all conference sports.

ARTICLE IX
ELIGIBILITY

Sec. 1 Eligibility shall be in accordance with the Ohio High School Athletic Association rules.

ARTICLE X
AMENDMENTS

Sec. 1 This constitution may be amended by a two-thirds vote of its membership.

Much of the work in any conference is done by the commissioner or executive secretary. It is most important to conduct all matters in a business-like way. This includes well structured agendas, minutes of meetings, reports, etc.

All conference scheduling, hiring of officials, and planning for meets involving member schools should be done well in advance.

ADVANCE PLANNING IN SCHEDULING

Every director of athletics should regulate his scheduling procedures in a precise and organized manner. One of the most satisfactory plans is to schedule for next year during that particular season. Many directors do not do this but wait until after the season is concluded. Schools that wait too long to prepare schedules have problems most difficult to solve.

A good rule of thumb to follow is to schedule one year in advance in all sports except varsity football. Here you should work at least two or three years in advance. The argument sometimes presents itself that you may be playing teams that could prove to be too strong if scheduling is too premature. This should be taken into consideration in any sport when scheduling—especially football.

There are some basic rules that can be quite beneficial in sound scheduling.

First—Make every effort to get a good balance of home and away games. This enables more uniform prices for season ticket sales and general income. It also keeps transportation costs in line.

Second—The director of athletics should plan his independent schedule in such a way that it has balance with the conference schedule.

Third—The type of competition should be given special consideration. Oftentimes teams are booked because of an attractive financial guarantee. As badly as most schools need the income, we must be careful not to get outclassed for the sake of revenue. This can result in an excess of injuries and a general tearing down of morale. This is especially true of early season football games where the teams are poorly matched. In an average season where the material is fair, your teams should play approximately .500. This too can be a good measuring stick to help determine your scheduling procedures.

Fourth—We should schedule teams that have a good following and can create a good rivalry if one does not already exist.

Fifth—We should use a similar philosophy in scheduling junior varsity and junior high school games. It is just as bad to play teams not comparable in competition at this level as in the varsity program.

Sixth—We should watch carefully the relationship that exists with the teams on our schedule, and should plan ahead accordingly. Areas such as good sportsmanship and crowd control deserve special attention.

Seventh—We must avoid competition that is too weak or too strong. Either extreme is wrong for obvious reasons. It is probably better to lose to a superior team than beat an inferior one in most cases if we must choose one or the other.

Eighth—We should expect first class treatment by the home school when we are playing away. In turn we should be good hosts to the visiting schools. There is really no alternative.

Ninth—Specific terms should be spelled out in contracts. This is especially true in sports involving ticket sales and gate receipts. It may also include provisions for hiring officials, game expenses, etc.

Shown in Figures 9-2 and 9-3 is a contract for athletic contests provided by the Ohio High School Athletic Association for use by its member schools. These contracts are made in duplicate and a copy is retained by each school. The back may be used for additional provisions not included on the face of the contract.

ASSIGNMENT OF OFFICIALS

One of the most exacting duties that faces every director of athletics deals with the hiring and assignment of officials. Emphasis on the quality of officials is too often either understressed or overstressed. Good officials are taken for granted, while poor ones are too often criticized by everyone but the concession stand employees who can't see the game.

It is most unfortunate to have a team practice all week for an important game, only to see the results greatly affected by poor officiating. It is equally poor to criticize officials for the outcome of games and for the calling of plays of a judgment nature.

The director of athletics must hire officials who are not only properly registered but who are really well qualified in their particular sport. What criteria should be followed in selecting these men?

First—We should employ officials who are in good standing with the district and state associations.

Second—We should hire men who like young athletes and who enjoy working with them in athletic competition.

HOME SCHOOL COPY

OHIO HIGH SCHOOL ATHLETIC ASSOCIATION

CONTRACT FOR OFFICIALS

....................OHIO ...., 19......

The.................... High School and ....
Official's Name and Address

...................., an official registered with the Ohio High School Athletic Association, hereby enter into the following agreement: The said official agrees to be present and officiate....................
Name of Sport

games or meets to be played with.................... High School

	Date	Hour	Place	Position	Fee and Expenses
1.					
2.					
3.					
4.					

1. If either of the contracting parties fails to fulfill the terms of this contract, except by mutual consent, a forfeiture of the fee stated above shall be paid by the offending party to the other party within five (5) days after the date set for the game in this contract. It is understood that there is a moral obligation as well as a contractual obligation to be considered in making and breaking of contracts. Where moral obligations are not mutually adjusted, the OHSAA reserves the right to review the facts and determine what these adjustments should be. Officials must be mutually agreed upon by both schools.
2. The said school will pay the said official the amount stated above for his services, provided that the obligation of the school ceases if and when the official ceases to be a registered official or if the contest is cancelled because of unfavorable weather, epidemics or other emergencies.
3. The Association reserves the right to drop an official whose dues are not paid, who is unfair and biased, whose conduct on or off the field or floor unfits him to act as an official, who does not comply with 4-meeting requirement and the official uniform prescribed by the OHSAA.
4. This contract must be returned no later than ____________ or it will become null and void.
Date

Principal____________________ Date signed____________, 19____

Official____________ Current Reg. No.________ Date signed____________, 19____

Figure 9-2

CONTRACT FOR ATHLETIC CONTESTS

HOME SCHOOL COPY

OHIO HIGH SCHOOL ATHLETIC ASSOCIATION

MEMBER NATIONAL FEDERATION OF HIGH SCHOOL ATHLETIC ASSOCIATIONS

______________, Ohio, ______________, 19____

This Contract is drawn under the supervision of the Ohio High School Athletic Association and must be used in arranging games participated in by schools of this Association.

THIS CONTRACT, Subscribed to by the Principals and Faculty Managers of the ______________ High School

and of the ______________ High School, is made for ________ games of ________ to be played as follows:

One game at ______________ on ______________ at ________ P. M.

One game at ______________ on ______________ at ________ P. M.

Do not use term "corresponding dates" — use specific dates.

All games to be played under the following stipulations:

The ______________ High School agrees to pay to the ______________ High School the sum of ______________ dollars ($________), and the latter school agrees that this sum shall cover all its claims arising by virtue of this contract, except as provided in Item 1 herein below set forth.

1. **If either party hereto fails to fulfill its obligation of any part of this contract, the defaulting party shall pay to the other party the sum of $ ________ as damages, which said sum must be accepted by the injured party as complete compensation for any damages it may have suffered, the remainder of the contract shall not be binding on either party, and the breach of said contract shall be reported to the Ohio High School Athletic Association.**
2. **Postponement cannot result in annulment except by mutual consent.**
3. **The constitution and rules of the Ohio High School Athletic Association are a part of this contract.**
4. **The suspension or termination of its membership in the State Association by either of the parties to this contract shall render this contract null and void.**
5. **It is urged that a suggested list of state approved officials be made on the back of this contract sheet and its duplicate. The principal of the visiting school should scratch the names of those not acceptable and number those acceptable in the order of preference on both the original and duplicate. All officials used in football and basketball games must be registered.**
6. **Interstate games should be scheduled on National Federation State High School Athletic Association contracts which may be obtained free of charge from the Ohio High School Athletic Association.**
7. **Unless otherwise specified, this contract shall call for a first team game.**
8. **This contract must be returned no later than ________ (Date) or it will become null and void.**

Principal	Faculty Manager or Athletic Director	School	State
Principal	Faculty Manager or Athletic Director	School	State

Figure 9-3

Third–We must be certain that the officials are prompt, reliable, and cooperative.

Fourth–We need officials who constantly keep the players and coaches informed of special situations or problems.

Fifth–We must employ men who are safety conscious and who are willing and able to assist in emergency situations. These areas may include fights between players, serious injuries, crowd control problems as they affect the game itself, etc.

Sixth–Officials should be well versed on the rules and interpretations of these rules.

Seventh–All officials should have the proper uniform, be clean and well shaven. Uniforms should be pressed and in good repair.

Eighth–We should engage officials who work hard and are in proper position when making calls.

Ninth–It is important to use younger officials in games with more seasoned men. Inexperienced officials should not be given varsity assignments unless there is an emergency. Officials must learn from working games in recreation programs, junior varsity and junior high games, scrimmages, etc. A totally inexperienced crew should never be employed at any level.

One of the older trends that is becoming more popular in senior high and junior high schools involves the hiring of officials who work in teams. This plan usually works very efficiently since these men normally have the same assignments each game and are familiar with the areas covered and normal procedures followed in game situations.

It is important for the director of athletics to give specific assignments to officials when more than one man is employed. This helps eliminate misunderstandings and confusion when officials arrive at the game. By having a prior assignment, officials in sports such as football may plan for special duties and situations for that particular game.

The employing of officials should follow a similar pattern as that of scheduling games. When games are scheduled officials should be assigned at approximately the same time. The type of man employed should be somewhat dependent on the game being played. For example, if two very strong teams are meeting, this would be a poor time to hire younger, less experienced men.

Along these same lines, if varsity football is scheduled two or three years in advance, officials for these games should be hired accordingly. Athletic directors who delay in employing officials frequently have difficulty getting the men they want. This often results in more time being spent to accomplish results that are not as desirable.

Head coaches should be consulted by the director of athletics when hiring officials, although the director of athletics must really make the final decision.

The same basic principles should apply in junior varsity and junior high games as well. These teams need the best men available and will usually play accordingly.

There is sometimes a tendency on the part of athletic directors to employ the same men for a number of games. This is not desirable for several reasons. It tends to put the officials in an awkward position and can cause opposing schools to be somewhat skeptical.

The following contract forms are used by member schools of the Ohio High School Athletic Association. These forms are prepared in triplicate. The officials keep one copy. The visiting school and the home school each receives a copy.

On occasion a letter may be used such as the one shown in Figure 9-4. The original is retained by the official and the copy is signed and returned to the director of athletics. This procedure enables an official to have several commitments included on one form. It does not allow for visiting school copies. This procedure should never be followed in varsity games for this reason.

Executive secretaries and league commissioners should work very closely with athletic directors in employing officials for conference games. Approval of these men should be given by member schools' athletic directors, who in turn should advise the commissioners of new officials capable of working these games.

The commissioners should hire sufficiently far in advance to be certain that good men are available for all games.

The question frequently comes up as to whether a commissioner should hire officials and then wait until Monday of that week for specific assignments. In my opinion this is good for the leading teams in that particular sport but for no one else. These games are important for all schools. As a consequence, good

Date

Mr. Ron Oaklief
7984 Columbia Rd.
Olmsted Falls, Ohio 44138

Dear Ron:

Listed below are your officiating assignments for the Berea City Schools Junior High basketball games for the __________ season:

At Ford Jr. High School on __________ with Middleburg Hts.–3:30 p.m. (Other official–B. Reynolds.)

At Ford Jr. High School–on __________ with Greenbriar–3:30 p.m. (Other official–J. Silliman.)

At Roehm Jr. High School–on __________ with Ford–4:00 p.m. (Other official–J. Silliman.)

These are for 8th and 9th grade games, and the fee will be $12.50.

Please keep the original, sign the carbon copy and return it to me at your earliest convenience.

Sincerely,

Bob Purdy,
Director of Athletics

RP/ab
encl.

Figure 9-4

officials should be working in all of the games. Considerable pressure can also be put on key officials on numerous occasions by following this procedure. Special attention should be given in assigning officials to games where great rivalries exist and games between schools in the same system or district.

TREATMENT AND COOPERATION WITH OFFICIALS

There is no excuse for poor treatment of officials or improper hospitality on the part of the home school. Areas such as proper police protection, meetings with officials before the games, and special dressing room facilities are covered in other chapters of this book.

Reports by officials to executive secretaries or commissioners of conferences should be made after each game. Improper treatment as well as good treatment of officials should be clearly spelled out. Specific instances as they pertain to coaches, fans, players, etc. are important. These reports should be reviewed by all member schools and made part of the conference business agenda.

Officials may report serious problems to the state association office. This is not recommended unless the local school situation remains below standard and no measures are taken to make the necessary improvements.

Proper communication with officials before and following games is most important. Special instructions should be conveyed by the director of athletics to the officials so that there is no confusion or misunderstanding regarding unusual circumstances or events.

RESPONSIBILITY FOR CHARTERING TEAM BUSES

The responsibility for chartering buses for teams is one that should be assumed by the director of athletics. It not only involves transportation but also includes safety features and public relations aspects.

It is most advantageous for the supervisor of transportation and the director of athletics to meet before each season begins. Common problems can be discussed and plans for the future can be made.

The director of athletics should furnish the supervisor of transportation with exact dates, destinations, loading points, departure times, etc. for each sport. In turn, he should receive a letter with at least two copies confirming these trips. The principal and head coach will be given the copies of this letter for their use. Separate letters should be typed for each sport.

Memoranda should be sent to head coaches periodically, reminding them of their responsibility in this regard. The following items should be included:

1) Orderly fashion for loading the bus, including equipment storage
2) Conduct of the players while passengers

3) General attitude of coaches and players toward the driver. This also includes assistance with directions, weather problems, etc.
4) Cleanliness of bus
5) Checking the bus when returning home, to make certain that no equipment was left behind or that no damage has been done.

Arrangements for meals before or after the games should also be made in advance. The bus driver should be invited to eat with the team.

A sample of a trip sheet to a particular game is shown in Figure 9-5. These are filled out by the director of athletics at least one week prior to the game.

POLICIES AND RULES FOR SPECTATOR BUSES

Rules and regulations for student spectator buses must be made available to the administration, teachers, and student body. These rules must be strictly enforced by the director of athletics. He should be very selective in choosing chaperones for these trips and communicate closely with them following each trip.

Rules and Regulations for Student Spectator Buses

1. All students riding buses must have a ticket purchased in advance.
2. No refunds on tickets will be given because of bad weather or similar situations. Students unable to go to the game may get a substitute but should notify the athletic director of the change.
3. Students must return on spectator bus on which they rode to the game. Anyone returning home by any other means will be denied student spectator bus privileges for the balance of the school year.
4. Each bus will be chaperoned by at least one adult. Teachers should be used if at all possible in this capacity.
5. Students who arrive late and have missed the bus will be given no refund.
6. Student game tickets should be purchased in advance if such a policy exists with the opposing school.

BEREA CITY SCHOOL DISTRICT
DEPARTMENT OF TRANSPORTATION

FIELD TRIP REQUEST FORM FOR USE OF SCHOOL BUSES

BUILDING____________________Date of Application________________
Group Requesting Transportation______________________________
Destination and Purposes of Trip______________________________
Total Number of Persons to be Transported______________________
Date of Proposed Trip________________Time of Departure________________
Time of Return____________________
Loading Point for Buses____________________________________
Names of Faculty Members in Charge____________________________
____

____
Signature of Person Making Request

1. Use of school buses is limited to participants in school approved activities.
2. Submit this form in triplicate to the Office of the Assistant Superintendent in charge of Instruction at least ten (10) days before date of proposed trip.
3. If approved one copy will be returned to the school and one copy forwarded to the Supervisor of Transportation at least five (5) days before date of trip.

REQUEST APPROVED: ______________________________
Principal or Supervisor

____
Assistant Superintendent–Instruction

Speedometer Reading________________Returning
Speedometer Reading________________Starting
Total__________________________

Time Returning to Garage______________
Time Leaving Garage__________________
Total__________________________

Figure 9-5

7. The director of athletics of the opposing school should be notified the day of the game as to how many buses to expect. Directions for drivers should also be made available.

8. Students must return to the buses immediately after the game. Chaperones must check to be certain that all students are present.
9. Rules for students while on the bus:
   1) No smoking or drinking.
   2) No swearing or throwing things out of the windows.
   3) No "horseplay" with other students.
   4) Approved signs on outside of buses.
   5) Organized cheering is encouraged.
10. Cheerleaders should ride the student spectator buses. The squad should be divided so that cheerleaders will be on all of the buses.
11. Additional chaperones should be available in the event of illness, injury, discipline problems, etc. No bus should be permitted to depart without a chaperone.
12. Chaperone should check bus before leaving and have driver verify O.K. condition.

TEN

Determining and Applying Dependable Day Game Procedures

Much preparation and planning is necessary when any interscholastic athletic event is being held. Most schools make an honest effort to do a good job at the games and meets where admissions are charged and when the attendance is good. Unfortunately the organization at many other events leaves much to be desired.

Too often the director of athletics will assign duties to the coaches themselves or others for game preparations when the real responsibility for these details should be assumed by the director himself. This may result in poorly handled preparations, or perhaps not even attempted.

Although practically all of the work is done well in advance of the scheduled game or meet, many last minute adjustments are necessary.

Basic Check List

Shown in Figure 10-1 is a typical varsity football game check list. Other items could be added if they seem especially important at a particular school or game site. This list should be thoroughly reviewed and verified, item by item, before coming to the game that night.

VARSITY FOOTBALL CHECK LIST

SIGNS											
MONEY											
GENERAL ADM. TICKETS											
RES. SEC. TICKETS											
PROGRAMS AND SELLERS											
TACKS, PENCILS											
PUNCHES, TAPE, HAMMER											
CHECKS–WORKERS AND OFFICIALS											
SEASON TICKETS											
PRESS BOX											
DOCTOR AND TRAINER											
STRETCHER											

Figure 10-1

Figure 10-1 *(con't.)*

USHERS											
GATE HELP											
TICKETBOARD											
ADULT AND STUDENT CAR PARKERS											
POLICE											
OFFICIALS											
PHONES											
CONCESSIONS											
	OPPONENT AND DATE	OPPONENT AND DATE	OPPONENT AND DATE								

The check list in Figure 10-1 is the one used by the Berea City Schools for home varsity football games.

For best results a faculty member or other competent adult should be in charge of a particular function. For example, one person should be responsible for the concessions stand operation, etc. Such an organization can allow the director of athletics to better supervise the many different activities which are taking place at each game or meet.

GATE HELP ASSIGNMENTS

One of the most important functions at any athletic event, where admission is charged, is the proper handling of the gates. These people are not only public relations representatives for the schools but at the same time must be firm, fair, and honest in ticket sales for all concerned.

It is my opinion that nearly all, if not all, of the faculty members interested in working at games be given assignments from time to time. The more experienced people should be given the critical areas and the better attended games. In most cases the women teachers are more competent at ticket selling and the men teachers at ticket-taking positions.

The ticket manager or faculty manager should be responsible for the gate help assignments and instructions. It is an excellent idea to meet at school several days prior to the first game with these teachers to properly instruct them in the different phases of their duties. A short meeting at the game site as they arrive for work can help clarify any last minute questions.

It is highly advisable to pay all game workers the same fee unless certain assignments require much more work or responsibility.

Ticketboards at each gate are extremely helpful. These should show samples of all presale student and adult tickets, adult and student season tickets, press-box passes, faculty passes, conference passes, etc. These sample tickets should also be classified in such a manner that the gate help will know whether to collect, check, or punch them.

A special policy should also be used for scouts from visiting schools. Many of them will have passes from their athletic directors. Others will show a conference pass from their respective league secretary. No scout should be admitted unless he is properly identified, or unless arrangements have been made prior to the game by his athletic director. Some schools will register scouts to help eliminate people who would normally pay from trying to gain free admission.

USHERS AND PROGRAM SELLERS

The work of ushers at athletic events will vary widely. The role they play will depend to a large degree on the facilities and on the type of game or meet that is being conducted. In most cases it is advisable to have ushers at any event where an admission is being charged.

In the average high school this responsibility may be assigned to the letterman's club, the Hi-Y, the Key Club (Junior Kiwanis Organization), or another service organization. They should be prompt, courteous, well-organized, and appropriately dressed. It is highly recommended that these ushers wear letter sweaters or jackets with insignia indicating the organization that they represent.

At football games or other outdoor activities where ushers may be needed, armbands indicating their duties can be extremely helpful.

In this category as in the many others, a teacher or sponsor should be in charge of this group and should be responsible for the discharge of their duties.

The question constantly comes up as to whether students who work at athletic events should be paid. In most schools the financial structure is such that the athletic departments cannot afford to pay for these services. A good policy to follow is to invite student workers to the appropriate athletic banquets and to properly acknowledge their services.

Sometimes their club treasury can be given a token amount from the athletic department. The direct payment for student game workers is not only costly but can create many problems.

The role of program sellers will vary considerably and will depend to a large extent on the athletic event being conducted. The selling of programs may not even be similar in schools within the same system or district.

Sometimes adult program sellers can do this work more satisfactorily and are less hesitant in "pushing their product." Regardless, this phase of the overall operation is extremely important.

Much time and effort has been spent in getting advertisements, patron listings, pictures, write-ups, etc. to make the program a worthwhile project. Considerable income can be realized by properly and systematically controlling program sales.

Here again a responsible adult must be in charge of this group. He must be certain that the program sellers are properly identified by appropriate jackets, hats, badges, or armbands. He should see that they are located at all gates and areas where the traffic pattern is heavy. They should have sufficient change and programs so that there is no delay at the busy time prior to the game. There must be an accounting of these funds by each seller and by the person in charge.

Student groups that sell programs at games may receive a percentage of their total sales. It is recommended that this money be transferred directly to that organization's account and not given to the students.

CITY POLICE

One of the most important aspects of any athletic event which is, well attended, or at which admission is charged, is the protection afforded by the city policy department. The number of officers requested for a particular game or meet will vary considerably. The part that they play in crowd control is most significant, and will be discussed in more detail in Chapter 11.

There are several points that can serve as effective guidelines for police protection at any event.

(1) Have an officer in charge of the police detail. They are to report directly to him for instructions and assignments.
(2) Report in proper uniform at the designated game site and at the requested time.
(3) Pre-game meeting with the officer-in-charge and the director of athletics to review the necessary procedures for that particular event.
(4) Role of the police in the event of militant demonstrations, serious athletic injuries, or other emergencies.
(5) Specific instructions for post-game plans. They can include traffic control, police protection for a dance following the game, parking lot assignments, spectator and team bus escorts, etc.

COOPERATION WITH OFFICIALS

The manner in which the athletic director treats game officials has a direct bearing on the reputation of the school and the athletic department. There is no excuse for poor hospitality under any circumstances. We must respect these men and cooperate with them at all times before, during, and after the contest.

It is most important that every official in every sport arrive at the game site at least forty-five minutes prior to the starting time.

We should provide reserved parking facilities for them if at all possible. If reserved parking is not available or not really necessary, the officials should be encouraged to park near the stadium or school where the game is being played.

If the officials bring members of their families with them, they should be admitted free and given good seats.

It is a good policy to meet the officials as they arrive and to escort them to their dressing room. Every effort should be made to provide a clean, well lighted, and properly ventilated dressing facility. Privacy is of the utmost importance and should be insisted upon. Clean towels and the game ball should be given to the officials shortly after their arrival.

After all of the officials have arrived and before they have started their own meeting to review their responsibilities for that particular game, the director of athletics should conduct a brief but thorough and well-organized meeting.

The following items are some of the most essential matters that should be considered at football games. Some of these may also apply to other events.

(1) Explain the procedure for handling serious injuries to players. If an ambulance is required, the officials should know who makes the call, where to have it enter the stadium, etc.

(2) The officials should know who the doctor in attendance will be and where he may be contacted during the game.

(3) The scoreboard operator should be introduced to the officials. The conference rules or game rules for that particular contest, as they pertain to the scoreboard, should be clarified. The plan to follow in the event of electrical difficulties with the scoreboard must be understood.

(4) The "chain-gang" (preferably adults dressed in appropriate uniforms) should be introduced to the officials. They in turn should discuss their role with the head linesman.

(5) The director of athletics should advise the officials of any special half-time programs such as parents' night, homecoming, booster nights, etc. In the event of a half-time extension, the officials and both teams should be contacted prior to the game regarding this matter.

(6) The officials should be given a key to lock their dressing room door or else be assigned someone responsible for this.

(7) Satisfactory arrangements for police protection should be completely understood.

The director of athletics should always meet with the officials following the game. If possible refreshments should be made available in the dressing room. The officials should be paid before leaving if they were employed by the director of athletics. If they were assigned to that game by the executive secretary of the conference, then the normal league policy will prevail.

TEAM PHYSICIAN AND TRAINER

The role of the team physician and trainer for any high school or junior high program is really twofold. First of all it gives the athletic director and coach the added assurance that injuries will be properly handled. Secondly, the public relations value alone is most significant. We don't have doctors in attendance at most of our football and wrestling practices. We oftentimes do not have a trainer available at practices. However, when game nights arrive, we are most anxious to have the proper medical care available.

At what events should we have a physician in attendance? The following list covers the minimum number of events for safety purposes.

(1) All football games–junior high school, junior varsity, and varsity games. The home school should be responsible for the physician in attendance. Varsity football teams should make an effort to take a physician with them to away games also.

(2) All basketball and wrestling tournaments. These should also include junior high through varsity high school competition.

(3) Large relay meets in track and swimming at all grade levels.

(4) If possible at all wrestling matches.

(5) At cheerleading and gymnastics clinics. Since it is not always possible to have a medical doctor at some of these events, a registered nurse may be used on occasion.

The team physician should attempt to follow the guidelines listed below when working at games.

(1) Arrive at the game being covered forty-five minutes early.
(2) Work closely with the trainer or coach responsible for taping and wrapping injuries.
(3) Be the final authority as to whether a boy who has been injured should play in the game.
(4) Be certain that splints, oxygen, stretcher, and other medical supplies are available. The trainer or coach should be responsible for these supplies and for their being made ready for the physician's use.
(5) Check on the availability of an ambulance or rescue truck from the fire department.
(6) Visit the home and opponent's locker rooms between halves and following the game to make certain all players are receiving proper care. In the event that they may require hospitalization for any period of time, he should make these arrangements with the coach and athletic director.

Because of the limited time that most physicians can give to the teams and sometimes at games, every effort should be made by the athletic director, coach and trainer to assist him in any way possible.

When scheduling physicians to work at games, it is highly recommended to give them as much advance notice as possible. This is most helpful for them in making their plans. Arrangements should also be made in the event that the regularly scheduled physician is unable to attend the game because of an emergency or some other problem.

Many schools do not have a regular trainer as such. Much of the work that must be done in the absence of a trainer can be the responsibility of an assistant coach or student trainer.

Special courses are offered that can be most beneficial to the student and coach alike. It is most important that any questionable matters be referred directly to the team physician.

At games where a doctor is in attendance, the trainer can serve as a valuable assistant in many matters. He can also learn much from the physician which can help him with his trainer's duties.

Shown in Figure 10-2 is an excellent check sheet prepared and used by Mr. Ron Culp, trainer at Baldwin-Wallace College in Berea, Ohio. This is specifically for away football games but may be adapted to other sports for traveling purposes and home games as well.

FOOTBALL TRUNK FOR GAMES AWAY

Tape ½ inch	12 rolls	Analgesic balm and packs
Tape 1 inch	1 can	Triangular bandages
Tape 1½ inch	1 can	Short air splint
Tape 2 inch	9 cans	Band aids and sterile guaze pads
Tape 3 inch	1 can	Paper cups
Tape stick and brush		Eye shadow
1 can Tuf-Skin		Firm grip (aerosal)
Elastic tape:	4 inch–1 can	Sprayhalant
	3 inch–1 can	Salt
	2 inch–4 rolls	Alcohol
Taping pads (Lisco and rubber)		Stockinette
Tape cutters–6		Diapers
2 inch guaze roller bandage–25		Ice bag
Adhesive felt and rubber		White gas
Elastic bandage– 6", 4", and 3"		Kling
Ankle wraps		Tongue blades
Vinyl–¼"-½"		Moleskin
Bruise and shin fiber pads		First aid cream
Sponge pads		Squeeze bottle
Knee cups		Shoe horn

CRUTCHES - PAILS - APRONS - PARING KNIFE - FOLDING TABLE
(if making a trip where facilities are not known)

Figure 10-2

CUSTODIAL RESPONSIBILITIES

The custodian at the stadium and school and the field maintenance men in all sports render a most valuable service. If they are well trained and capable in their work, they are the equivalent to an assistant athletic director.

Most of the ineffective groundskeepers and custodians have little training or direction in their particular positions when it pertains to athletics. This is partially the fault of the athletic director, who must help assume this responsibility. Some of the work not done on the fields or in the gymnasium can easily be corrected.

The athletic director must exercise a more positive and helpful attitude in advising these men as to what is really expected of them.

Mr. Rex Smith, the highly competent director of athletics for the Parma City Schools (the largest suburban system in Cleveland) has devised an excellent checklist (Figure 10-3) for field maintenance men. This is specifically for home football games but could be easily adapted to other sports as well.

ROLE OF THE CHEERLEADERS

Although the cheerleader program is covered in detail in Chapter 14, the role that they play in game day procedures is well worth mentioning.

First, they should be most instrumental in arrangements for the pep assemblies. The people involved the format to be followed, and other such details must be planned and then approved by the cheerleader coach and athletic director and principal.

Second, prompt arrival at the games at predetermined times is most important. Cheerleaders may often be used to assist as ushers, program sellers, gate help, or other similar duties on a temporary basis until other arrangements can be made.

Third, cheerleaders should be well versed in the part that we expect them to play in crowd control matters. They can be most influencial in promoting good sportsmanship, especially in the student sections.

Fourth, cheerleaders can assist the athletic director with some of the details on special occasions such as homecoming, parents' night, boosters' night, etc. They can present the mothers with mums and the dads with numbers corresponding to their sons' uniform numbers. They also are helpful at decorating, putting up signs for special sections, etc.

Fifth, cheerleaders can serve as hosts with refreshments following the games. They can do much to help the visiting team and home school to breach any ill feelings resulting from the game.

PARMA PUBLIC SCHOOLS
Parma, Ohio

BYERS FIELD FOOTBALL PREGAME CHECK LIST

1. *Field*

a. Properly marked–yellow goal line
b. Corner flags set properly
c. Team benches
d. Check for low spots and fill in
e. Rope off section on west track 30 to 30 yard line
f. Lock all field entry gates except team and band entry gates
g. Stretcher at each team bench
h. American Flag

2. *Stadium*

a. Lock all perimeter gates and close off garage
b. Empty trash cans
c. Public, team and officials' toilet room–clean resupply with toilet paper, towels, soap and empty waste containers. Check light bulbs.
d. Ticket booths–clean, burn ticket stubs, clean counter, check lights. Save all parking and ticket admission signs. Dispose of all programs.
e. Team and officials' rooms–clean chalk boards and training tables. Provide chalk and erasers and provide soap (liquid or bar). Five chairs in officials' room.
f. Hot water for teams, officials and concession stands
g. Fly pennants on top of press box
h. Barricade at entrance to Board of Education Office–Ridge Road
i. Clean bleachers, press box and camera booth.

3. *Audio and Video*

a. PA set in press box
b. Field microphone
c. Phone in press box
d. Phone in officials' room
e. Byers Field phone system (Press box, east and west concession stands and ticket booth.)
f. Field phones
g. Portable, power megaphone
h. Singer for National Anthem
i. Video set up.

Figure 10-3

Figure 10-3 *(continued)*

4. *Lights*

   a. Field and crowd
   b. Outdoor floodlights on Board of Education roof coping
   c. Team, officials, toilet, ticket and concession areas
   d. Ramps under stands, vending areas and B & C ramps
   e. Scoreboard

Supply Items

Downsmarker and chains
Corner flags
Benches
Field phones and field "mike"
Stretcher
Chalk and erasers
Extra hand towels
Extra toilet paper
Extra bar soap
Game balls
Ball pump and extra needles
Officials jackets for downs crew
Towels for officials
School pennants
Hurdles and rope–west track
Record player and records
Fire extinguisher in concession stands
Oxygen units
Portable power megaphone
2-wheel truck
Towels for concession stand
Chalk and erasers

Additional check items

Programs
Field doctor
Officials assigned to their positions

Note: Any items found in stand or field clean-up are to be returned to the Athletic Office.

BAND PARTICIPATION

The role of the marching band in planning for games is too often minimized by the director of athletics. He often assumes that all necessary preparations have been made by his own band director and then coordinated with the visiting school. Too many things can go wrong if there is no organized procedure to follow. This is especially true since it affects the teams and officials as well.

For best results the director of athletics and the band director should consider the function of the band in three principal areas.

First is the pre-game schedule. The following items should be carefully planned:

(1) Practice before the game by the home school's band.
(2) Meeting the visiting school's band. Arrangements for bus parking and gates for admission.
(3) Time for taking the field for the pre-game show by both bands.
(4) Time and procedure for the National Anthem.
(5) The part that the band will play, if at all, in the introduction of players.
(6) Time for leaving the field so as not to delay the kick-off.
(7) Necessary arrangements for special seating sections for both bands.

Second is the half-time show. The following items should be well planned and organized in advance.

(1) Exact time remaining in the half when bands should start toward the field.
(2) Police assistance with the band as it enters the field.
(3) Prior arrangements as to the time allowed each band and other items pertaining to the half-time activities.
(4) Necessary provisions for a half-time extension with the director of athletics.
(5) Assist with special nights such as homecoming, parents' night, and other similar events.

Third is the post game plan. This part that the marching bands play is often neglected. The following details should be considered.

(1) Marching on the field following the game.
(2) Refreshments for the bands.
(3) Police protection or escort to the band buses.
(4) Proper traffic control for bus deployment.

ELEVEN

Utilizing Police Protection and Crowd Control Effectively at Athletic Events

The problem of crowd control at high school and junior high school athletic events is of one great concern throughout the nation. This topic appears on nearly every program that is presented at athletic director's meetings on district, state, regional, and national levels.

Superintendents, principals, boards of education, and state athletic associations are equally concerned over these pressing issues. The very existence of interscholastic athletics depends on proper planning and procedures for such contests.

The National Council of Secondary School Athletic Directors, a structure of the Division of Men's Athletics of the American Association for Health, Physical Education, and Recreation, released a publication in August of 1970 entitled "Crowd Control For High School Athletics." The author of this book served as the chairman of the committee to prepare this manual.

Much of the material in this chapter is taken from this publication.

A PLANNED PROCEDURE

Mr. Robert Wirth, stadium manager of the Parma City Schools in Parma, Ohio, has developed an excellent plan for what he appropriately refers to as crowd accommodation. These procedures are:

1. Crowd Control Procedures Prior to the Event.

Many weeks, even months, prior to the event of concern, whether it be football, basketball, wrestling, soccer, baseball, etc., the groundwork must be laid for the proper handling of all particulars that go into making up a successful game. Many weeks prior to a game date contacts should be made with the local police, sheriff's department or state patrol, etc. Areas to be discussed are as follows:

1. Traffic flow to the game
2. Traffic flow around the area during the game
3. Traffic flow away from the game
4. Police security plans to be in effect before, during, and after the game
5. Provisions for ambulance runs to and from the area
6. Posting of traffic directional signs, posting of No Parking signs
7. Other factors which may affect traffic flow
8. Pedestrian flow
9. Stores or businesses that may be adversely affected by crowds or traffic
10. Police cooperation and participation
11. Establishment of a pay scale for police if necessary.

Situations may vary as to the involvement of policy and police departments; however, a good security plan that spells out duties, times, conditions, and anything else that pertains to the safety of people is probably the most important facet of crowd control.

Much attention should be given to tickets for it is a known fact that a ticket to a very popular event not only is a ticket of admission but is an instrument of prestige. Therefore, the prestige factor as well as the advertising factor of an event can be capitalized on if a ticket is designed to be attractive, is designed to be informative, and is designed to advertise the event. Much time and effort should be put into this because this is one of the prime advertising preparations of your event. Care should be given to numbering of tickets and keeping adequate and accurate records.

In planning an event well ahead of the scheduled date, it is wise to have an alternate plan of refunding money or tickets in the event that there is a postponement after the crowd has arrived.

It is a very good idea many weeks prior to an event to arrange suitable advertising which will help in the promotion of the sport involved, the particular event, and the desired outcome, i.e., "good sportsmanship," "may the best team win," good wholesome recreation, good family recreation, etc. *Too many times advance publicity creates a hostile audience.* This can be controlled to some extent through planning the publicity well in advance of the event and coordinating this with the parties involved such as opposing teams, opposing schools, etc.

Several weeks prior to a particular season it is a good policy to meet with the news media to lay the groundwork for game reporting, public information, ticket information, and other things in which the news media might be interested.

Prior to the season in question the physical facilities of your field, arena or gym should be checked and rechecked, for if we talk of crowd accommodation, we must be ready with the facilities necessary for accommodating a large group of people. There must be adequate washroom space; it must be clean, well-lighted, and well-maintained. Broken seats, steps, screens, windows, etc. should be in the best of repair, and if at all possible your planned traffic flow within your arena, stadium, or gym should be well directed with the use of large signs well above head level. All washrooms should be clearly marked. All ramps, exits, entrances should be well marked with large signs. It is a good idea that a standard color and size be adopted for all signs at a particular field. This, in effect, educates people to the fact that if they see a particular sequence of colors, this is a sign which gives information in reference to direction of seating, rest rooms, or other information needed by the spectators.

Much of the outward success of an event can be measured directly by the ticket sales. Therefore, it would seem prudent to have someone spend some time and effort in this direction. The planning of ticket sales and the planning of so-called gimmick items to sell tickets are all part of sound game procedures that would take place prior to an event.

One should not overlook adequate means to contact the public for the purpose of selling tickets, as well as providing adequate facilities at a game for the purpose of selling tickets. These facilities ideally should be located some distance from the exists and entrances for two reasons:

1. The people arriving at the event who already hold tickets should not be held up by ticket lines.
2. People who are purchasing their tickets at the game will not create large crowds around the entrances.

Although this may not seem important, *the orderly flow of people into an event will very often set the tone which will be the basis for a crowd's reaction during the event.*

2. Procedures During the Event

Procedures to be followed during an event logically should start six to eight weeks prior to the actual beginning of the game, and it is at this time that a pre-game checklist should be used to keep track of and to check items and work that should be completed prior to the actual start of the event.

It is possible that several pre-game checklists would be necessary. A suggestion might be:

1. A pre-game checklist for the athletic director.
   A. This would include his duties, preparation, etc.
   B. His responsibilities prior to the game.
2. Field maintenance man or custodian.
   A. Preparation
   B. Duties
3. Man in charge of ticket sales.
   A. Duties
   B. Responsibilities
4. Timer and scorekeeper.
   A. Duties
   B. Responsibilities

A pre-game checklist would not necessarily be the same for all schools or all field houses. However, a good pre-game checklist can and should be developed before and after your first contests so that this can be put into effect 100 percent for future events.

During the event continual surveillance should be maintained on all facilities that pertain to crowd convenience or comfort such as concession stands, drinking fountains, first aid stations, washrooms, aisleways, etc. The importance of this is from the standpoint that a person leaving his seat to go to a washroom or the concession stand may become involved in a line or waiting period, and consequently he becomes angry and could become a potential problem later on in the game. Attempts should be made to eliminate all lines of people waiting for any purpose.

It is a good idea to keep small groups of people on the move or in seats. This should not be done with a display of police force, but rather as an established plan within the confines of your football field or gym whereby people become *educated to the fact* that they are there to watch an event that takes place on the playing field or floor, and loitering at the concession stand or underneath the stands will not be tolerated. This should be put into effect at your very first event and continued throughout the season. *This is a matter of crowd education.* It will be an expected behavior if established early in the season.

It is of great importance to have a security plan well worked out with the local police authorities and in the hands of the men in charge of the police contingent at your field or event. All police should be aware of this plan and any special phases of it. This includes providing immediate police help in the event of an injury, an ambulance coming on the field and leaving, and most important, a procedure to follow in the event of a person or persons being apprehended for various reasons within the confines of the field, fieldhouse, or gymnasium.

In the event of some trouble, if at all possible, the persons in question should be moved immediately and courteously into a closed room or other area out of sight of the general crowd. At this time steps can be taken to ascertain what might have caused any problem. By removing the person from the sight of the crowd you will minimize other action which might occur or be planned to occur.

If need be the people in question can then be removed by police car to the local police station for further questioning or other police procedures. However, it is not recommended that every case of this type be taken to the police station.

It is a good policy to keep all artificial noisemakers from coming through the ticket gate, as well as confetti and other things of this type. This would also exclude all beverages that might be in bottles, cans, or paper cartons, as these can become weapons or projectiles. There should be a suitable place for people to check these outside of the gate where they can be picked up after the game if needed. Here again, putting this into practice from the very first game on will *educate the crowd* as to things which are acceptable and things which are not. In the event that the prohibition of noisemakers, drinks, bottles, etc. should cause a fan to question your authority or reason for doing this, be very willing to refund the full purchase price of the tickets.

Constantly during the game it should be the responsibility of someone to continually check gates, ticket windows, concession stands, placement of police, press box facilities, washrooms, etc. If a fan is fully accommodated at an event there is no cause or reason for any abnormal type behavior, and it is the desirable type behavior for which we strive.

Special attention should be given to the last five minutes of the event. Under no circumstances should the ticket gates be open for anyone to come in at a reduced rate or at no fee or without a ticket. This again falls under the area of *crowd education.* It will eliminate people hanging around outside ticket windows and gates until such time as they can come in at a reduced rate. Charge the full price right up to the last second of the game. Generally speaking, the police and others, such as ushers, charged with keeping aisles open, should move from their position to a position where they can facilitate the orderly flow of people from the stands to the exits. Within two minutes of the end of the game all exits should be open but should not be left unattended. It is a good policy at the end of every event to have a somewhat sobering announcement made relative to pedestrian and traffic safety, such as, "May we have your attention, please. When leaving the game tonight, we hope you will not become a statistic–drive carefully" . . . "The streets are wet and slippery, please drive carefully" . . . "May we have your attention, please. We would like to have you back next week. Please drive carefully," or some other suitable announcement of this type.

3. Procedures After the Event

In reference to spectator education it is a good idea to put various plans into action immediately following a game. One such plan would be to start turning out field lights as soon as it is feasibly possible. This indicates to the crowd that you are closing up and it is time for them to leave. Your field maintenance man or custodian should immediately, at the end of the game, start to collect all field markers, flags, and any other equipment which is on the field. If the event is indoors suitable action should be taken.

It is a good idea to keep the man on your public address system working until most of the crowd has left. He should be at the P.A. system and available to make any type of emergency announcement.

In the event that visiting spectators arrived at the field in buses, it is an excellent plan to have the buses under surveillance before, during, and after the game. This can be accomplished by moving some of the uniformed policemen from the field to the buses immediately following the game. These men would augment the people assigned the surveillance before and during the game.

If pre-game planning were sufficient and a suitable security plan was adopted, the traffic flow away from the field should be fast and in a specific direction.

Satisfactory methods of crowd control will dictate that masses of people moving in one direction generally will not result in altercations of any type. One way traffic leaving an event will move quickly and with a minimum of trouble, and this should be spelled out in detail with your local police department and should be handled by them.

It is a good idea to have help in parking lots to facilitate the moving of cars onto highways. It is also a good idea immediately following an event to have assigned policemen moving with the crowd out to parking areas or bus areas, or areas where many people will pass. In this fashion a man in uniform is again always in sight, and, hence, is a deterrent to any abnomral behavior.

A possible source of further trouble after the game or event is the visiting team locker room or the home team locker room, especially when the teams come out and head for their buses or cars. It is wise to keep both teams apart if at all possible, or if time and funds permit, it is an excellent idea to bring both teams together in an atmosphere of sportsmanship and fellowship if food and refreshments could be provided when they finish dressing.

Uniformed police should be in the area of team buses at all times after the game to help these buses leave the area and prevent any unforeseen occurrence which might create ill feelings on the part of the visiting school. An hour or so after an event it is wise to check with the local police authorities to determine if any unforeseen things happened such as fights, auto accidents, property damage, etc. within the immediate area surrounding the field or gym. The reason for this is to obtain information which might be incorporated into your after game plans or your security plan that would act as a preventative measure for future occurrences of this type. This would seem to be a sound public relations type procedure and, of course, is aimed at prevention rather than the cure. Once adverse crowd behavior gains public attention it is extremely difficult, if not impossible, to erase this from the minds of the public, especially if it hits the newspapers in a sensational manner. Good public relations never hurt any athletic program. Good public relations are earned by satisfactory planning and implementing these plans so as to please and accommodate the visiting public as well as those who might live in the surrounding area.

The Law and the Spectator

Many questions arise concerning the status and legal rights of spectators at athletic contests. Professor Howard C. Leibee of the Physical Education Department at the University of Michigan has researched this particular topic in depth. Some of his findings follow:

I. LEGAL STATUS OF THE SPECTATOR

A. Right to Admission

1. A public agency may refuse to admit a person to an activity for good cause only, and may not make arbitrary or individious discriminations. Evidence of past misconduct on the premises or evidence that admission would jeopardize safe conduct of the event

may suffice. *Tamellee v. New Hampshire Jockey Club, Inc.* 163 A 2d 10 (1960).

2. If it is impossible to accommodate persons who hold tickets, the agency must refund the price of the tickets or supply other seats at the same price.
3. "Where a mistake is made in selling tickets for seats already sold, the management should, in a polite and courteous manner, offer to refund the price of tickets or supply other seats at the same price; and, if this is done and the ticket holders refuse to accept the seats, no right of action accrues to them." 86 Corpus Juris Secundum, S 32 Theatres and Shows, p. 711. In support of that position, the cases of *Powell v. Weber-Stair Co.*, 125 S.W. 255, and *Weber-Stair Co., v. Fisher*, 119 S.W. 195, are cited.

II. STATUS OF THE TICKET BUYER

A. Once he has been admitted and seated, the ticket-buying spectator is clothed with a particular legal status which governs the actions and responsibilities of the "proprietor" toward him.

B. The courts seem to be split on whether the paying spectator is an "invitee"[1] (Defined as "one who is invited or remains upon the premises, for a purpose which concerns the business of the invitor") or a "licensee"[2] ("One who stands in no contractual relationship to the owner or occupier of premises, but is permitted or tolerated thereon, expressly, impliedly, or inferentially, merely for his own interest, convenience, or pleasure, or for that of a third person"). 53 *Corpus Juris Secundum,* S 79, P. 807.

1. *Ivory v. Cincinnati Baseball Club Co.*, 24 N.E. 2d 837 (1939), and *James v. Rhode Island Auditorium, Inc.*, 199 A. 293
2. Marrone v. Washington Jockey Club, 227 U.S. 633 (1913).

Duty Owed to Invitees and Licensees

1. One court has expressed the duty of the invitor to the invitees as a requirement to "exercise ordinary

care to guard them against danger, and to that end he must exercise ordinary care to render the premises reasonably safe for the invitees." *Ivory,* supra, at 839.

2. Toward a licensee, the proprietor owes only the duty to warn off hazardous conditions and to refrain from acts of active negligence, wanton and willful conduct, and gross negligence. See James, "Tort Liability of Occupiers of Land: Duties Owed to Licensees and Invitees," 63 *Yale L.J.* 605 (1954).
3. It has been said that the duty of the manager of an enterprise extends to maintaining order on the premises, including responsibility for the conduct of their parties,[1] and that in discharge of the obligation of reasonable care, the manager is required to take action only when he has reason to expect, from what he has observed or from past experience, that the conduct of the third person will be dangerous to others.[2]
   1. *Planchard v. Klaw* and *Erlanger New Orleans Theatre Company,* 166 La. 235, 117 So. 132 (1928).
   2. Prosser, *Cases and Materials on Torts,* 4th ed. 1967, P. 517, Note 2.
4. It has been held that there is a duty to remove disorderly, intoxicated persons. *Martin v. Philadelphia Gardens,* 348 Pa. 232, 35 A. 2d 317.

D. Statutes in some states (for example, Kansas Statutes annotated 72-1033) place control of school facilities and property in the hands of the school board, and "(w)here an athletic field is located on property owned by a school district, the management and control of such field are vested in the officers of the school board. . . . ". See 78 Corpus Juris Secundum, Schools and School Districts, Section 251, p. 1220, and *Nieman v. Common School Dist. No. 95, Butler County,* 232 p. 2d.

E. From the above, it follows that the agency (for example, school district) ultimately responsible for conducting and supervising the event is under a legal duty to provide for the safety of the spectators through provision for all foreseeable circumstances. This duty encompasses control of the crowd and individuals, and failure to carry out that duty adequately may render the agency and/or individuals liable for injuries resulting from that failure negligently caused.

III. STATUS OF THE COMPLIMENTARY TICKET HOLDER

A. Since the grant of a complimentary ticket may be deemed an express invitation, the holder of the ticket occupies the status and rights of an invitee. (Refer to II C, 1)

B. Circumstances under which the ticket was received by the holder bears strongly on final determination of his status, in the event of litigation.

IV. STATUS OF THE GATE CRASHER

A. Since the gate crasher has no legal right, permission, or invitation to be on the premises, he may be treated as a trespasser. Generally speaking, there is a right to remove or request his removal from the premises.

B. Duty owed to trespassers

1. The trespasser takes the conditions as he finds them, and no duty toward him (on the part of the proprietor) arises until he is discovered. Even then, the duty is only to make a reasonable effort to keep him from harm.
2. If force is used to effect his removal, only that amount of force which is necessitated by the circumstances will be permitted. *Gorman v. United Theatres,* (La. App.) 177 So. 463.

C. Recommendations:

1. Use reasonable measures designed to prevent entry of gate crashers and to discover them promptly, such as patrolling areas where entry could be made.
2. Eject gate crashers promptly after discovery, avoiding possible unruly involvement in chasing persons

through a crowd, in order to minimize occurrence of incidents likely to arouse the interest of the crowd.

3. In removing a gate crasher, use only that amount of force demanded by his conduct.

Community Involvement

The need and value of a good interscholastic athletic program is recognized by nearly every community. As a result the community itself is willing to work through the school officials and police to help with crowd control problems.

The city of Toledo, Ohio is an excellent example of this involvement. Mr. Hilton Murphy, Commissioner of Athletics and Community Relations for the Toledo Public Schools, Dr. Frank Dick, Superintendent of Schools in Toledo, and Deputy Police Chief Erwin Oehlers of the Toledo Police Department have combined with many community groups to preserve the athletic program in that city. This was a program that was nearly destroyed by destructive youth gangs.

Part of Mr. Murphy's program of community involvement follows:

Guidelines, to be effective, must involve the public by teaching them what we are trying to achieve in our educational objectives of the athletic program. Involvement of Boosters Clubs and parent groups can be a positive factor in crowd control. Effective leadership in organization will aid in the good sportsmanship part of athletic events. As a result we must create an awareness within organizations of the school, the district, and the league in the city as to the rules and policies of the athletic program. This awareness can be helped by discussions at meetings of organizations, the rules and regulations of various sports, how to maintain permanent liasion between school administration and these organizations, and to explain and discuss the roles and duties of crowd control personnel. Resource people should be assigned to send letters to parents explaining the problem of crowd control and encouraging positive and supportive attitudes.

For the protection of the game, the future should probably focus on less paid uniformed off duty police at a game and more paid boosters members at a given game, because people selected from the community have become more effective in handling emotional crowds and police less effective, the idea here being that the students know the adults and have some respect for the adults who live within their own community. A mixture of policemen and Boosters Clubs and interested adults concerned about the school itself will go a long way in keeping some of the disorders down and putting out brush fires before they become major confrontations. This all comes under the heading of community involvement.

Developing of a working relationship with city officials helps in many ways to establish a liasion with the agency that supplies the control services, such as the police, the detectives, the police community relations and the courts, and the fire department. It is important to get these people involved to attend these meetings of the city governmental bodies and keep officials aware and informed of crowd control measures and problems.

Another important point is to inform the news media what is going on—or what could happen—and after something does happen to be honest and explain exactly what happened. Too many school officials try to sweep disturbances and incidents under the rug and then have the news media pull the rug out from under them. It is better to be honest with the news media and let them decide what to print and not to print than to try to hide something that comes out in an ugly story later. Community leaders and agencies and school officials should all be given some type of crowd control procedure brochure which involves and tells how the community would be involved in problems of the schools. Police, school security duties should be pinpointed in crowd control of stadiums and police school gymnasium security agreement should be made in basketball procedures. Responsibilities must be pinpointed. Excuses after something happens cannot be tolerated in society today. Sportsmanship programs should be arranged within the schools where referees, coaches, police, and observers rate the student and adult and team behavior at games and when these results are controlled. It tends to give focus to the fact that sportsmanship is a definite goal of the school. The interchange of cheerleaders and team captains at pep meetings the day of the game all helps to get the two schools involved in a good frame of mind for the contest. Public address systems at games should also stress good sportsmanship.

Community involvement should be organized by the various service clubs to have members speak to the young athletic groups especially. Officials should be carefully selected and placed in games in which the official can definitely handle a situation as it might be presented.

Finally, the entire community should get behind the idea of developing in our young people the over-all respect of law and authority. This is necessary if our athletic programs are to be saved for students who do appreciate it.

THE "SUPPORTIVE" PEOPLE

The role and responsibility of the "supportive" people in crowd control is most significant. Many groups and organizations may contribute to help assure orderly conduct on the part of spectators and participants as well.

ATHLETIC DIRECTORS

1. Review checklist of game management responsibilities.
2. Explore ideas, circumstances, and guidelines with other schools at league meetings.
3. Assign experienced staff personnel at vulnerable stations.
4. Review station, or gate, assignments thoroughly with staff prior to each game.
5. Review with Police Supervisor special information and/or assignments prior to each game.
6. Check with police and gate supervisors at half time.
7. Utilize morale building organizations–Parents' Clubs, Varsity Clubs, Pep Clubs, etc.
8. Announce over the P.A. System the policy that no unauthorized spectators are allowed on the field prior to, or during, a game.
9. Schedule pre-season assemblies to review rules and discussions of good sportsmanship and spectator behavior . . . as often as necessary thereafter.
10. Provide for a planned check of facilities and area in vicinity of school after contests.

COACHING STAFF

1. Work with the Principal and the Athletic Director in

conducting assemblies to inform students of rules, conduct, and sportsmanship.

2. Set an influential tone of conduct, visibly showing the value of self restraint, fair play, and sportsmanlike conduct.
3. Remove from the game any trouble makers and players who display unsportsmanlike gestures.
4. Have a concern for personal appearance and good taste in personal grooming by all squad members.
5. Be a vigorous, forceful, and inspiring personality—"Be a leader of boys and a builder of men."
6. Avoid demonstrations, or irritations, which may result in excessive excitement, or antagonizing of the crowd.

PLAYERS

1. Act like an athlete . . . a gentleman.
2. Display mutual respect at all times.
3. Avoid show-boating, unsportsmanlike gestures, and harassing opponents and officials.
4. Concentrate on the game and take little notice of the audience.
5. Cooperate with officials.
6. Influence spectators by your good conduct.
7. Display a concern for and assist an injured opponent if the situation presents itself.
8. Congratulate a team for its performance.

CHEERLEADERS

1. Stimulate and control crowd response.
2. Choose the right cheers at the right time.
3. Care should be taken in making certain that words used in a cheer are not suggestive or do not inflame an audience.
4. "Welcome" yells are appropriate.
5. Cheers should be under the leadership of the cheerleaders.
6. Avoid the use of bells, horns, and noisemakers.
7. Gestures of cheerleaders should be synchronized, pleasing to watch, and easy to follow.

8. Divert the crowd's attention by starting a popular yell when booing develops.
9. Respect visitors–eliminate competition between cheerleading by not conducting a cheer at the same time as the visiting cheerleading squad.
10. Be organized and prepared.

OFFICIALS

1. Maintain a neat and creditable appearance.
2. Know fully the rules and accepted officiating procedures.
3. Make decisions promptly . . . fairly . . . without arrogance.
4. Be consistent.
5. Eliminate officiating show-boating.
6. Be on time and start the game on time.
7. Refrain from placing hands on players during an athletic contest.
8. Be dignified, but never cocky.
9. Be together with working officials. . . . A pre-game conference prior to each game is helpful.
10. Be friendly, but businesslike.

Responsibilities of the State and National Associations

Dr. Harold Meyer, Commissioner of the Ohio High School Athletic Association, wrote a chapter in the manual entitled "Crowd Control for High School Athletics," prepared by the National Council of Secondary School Athletic Directors. He discussed the responsibilities that state and national associations must exercise in administering high school athletic programs.

A portion of his contribution to this manual follows:

Every state in the union, including the District of Columbia, has some type of association that is directly involved in the administration of high school athletics. A number of states include athletics along with other extra-curricular activities while other states have separate associations for non-athletic activities.

Since the organization is already present, it is imperative that each state association adopt rules and regulations governing the conduct of athletic contests under its jurisdiction.

Such rules and regulations may be a part of the association's constitution and by-laws or be promulgated through bulletins, news letters or other media.

All schools must be made aware that they have certain required responsibilities as a member of the association, as a host school or as a visiting school. The responsibility may vary in degree, but not in importance.

Crowd control is a problem only if there is a crowd and the assumption is being made that an athletic contest of some sort was responsible. Since the athletic event was the cause it then becomes the logical point to start in the establishment of controls.

To insure the correct behavior of student athletes it should be mandatory that a faculty member of the school should accompany the team or individuals to athletic contests. This person could be a coach, teacher or the administrative head of the school. His duties will vary with the type of activity, but primarily he is the person of responsibility.

Some athletic rule books contain certain rules that govern the actions of coaches while a contest is in progress. The rule makers may have had the protection of the officials in mind, but indirectly the rules have had some effect on the behavior of the crowd. Some rules provide a yardage penalty, as in football, a free throw in basketball, or a loss of a team point in wrestling. In some cases, a coach may be ejected from the area of the contest if he persists in such unsportsmanlike behavior. Since all penalties are assessed by game officials it is important that a complete report be made to the state association for any follow-up deemed necessary. Some states impose a monetary penalty on the coach or school, others may invoke probation or suspension upon the school if the conditions were considered serious enough.

Most coaches realize that their sideline actions have a decided effect on the attitude of the team followers and govern themselves accordingly. For the few coaches, however, that do not assume this responsibility, provisions should be made for some type of control, or penalty, other than the penalties incurred in the game itself.

The Fundamentals of Sportsmanship

1. SHOW RESPECT FOR THE OPPONENT AT ALL TIMES

The opponent should be treated as a guest; greeted cordially on arriving; given the best accommodations; and accorded the tolerance, honesty, and generosity which all human beings deserve. Good sportsmanship is the Golden Rule in action.

2. SHOW RESPECT FOR THE OFFICIALS

The officials should be recognized as impartial arbitrators who are trained to do their job and who can be expected to do it to the best of their ability. Good sportsmanship implies the willingness to accept and abide by the decisions of the officials.

3. KNOW, UNDERSTAND AND APPRECIATE THE RULES OF THE CONTEST

A familiarity with the *current* rules of the game and the recognition of their necessity for a fair contest is essential. Good sportsmanship suggests the importance of conforming to the spirit as well as the letter of the rules.

4. MAINTAIN SELF CONTROL AT ALL TIMES

A prerequisite of good sportsmanship requires one to understand his own bias or prejudice and the ability to prevent the desire to win from overcoming rational behavior. A proper perspective must be maintained if the potential educational values of athletic competition are to be realized. Good sportsmanship is concerned with the behavior of all involved in the game.

5. RECOGNIZE AND APPRECIATE SKILL IN PERFORMANCE REGARDLESS OF AFFILIATION

Applause for an opponent's good performance is a demonstration of generosity and good will that should not be looked upon as treason. The ability to recognize quality in performance and the willingness to acknowledge it without regard to team membership is one of the most highly commendable gestures of good sportsmanship. With the fundamentals of sportsmanship as the point of departure, specific responsibilities and expected modes of behavior can be defined.

TWELVE

Designing a Balanced System for Honoring Athletes and for Developing Girls' Interscholastic Athletics

Every sport in every athletic program is important. We must believe this or they should not be included in our department. Since this is true, we must be certain that our program is designed in such a manner as to have good balance in conducting each activity.

A good athletic department today must also include a new and progressive girls' interscholastic program. Because of financial problems, lack of facilities, and general indifference, the girls' program has not made the progress that is inevitable.

This chapter will attempt to stress the importance of all sports being offered.

BASIC POLICY FOR BANQUETS

The basic policy for senior high school athletic banquets seems to be one that is always being discussed and one that is not easily resolved. The idea of one large all sports banquet in the spring is still employed by some systems. Few individuals can really be properly recognized at these banquets. Fall and winter seasons are nearly forgotten. The program is so large, justice can hardly be done to any team.

Individual banquets for each sport is not good either. This tends to divide the program—to work one against the other. It also means arrangements for nine or ten separate programs. The one really good outcome of this plan is the brevity of the program since only one sport is involved.

Probably the best plan (and they all have weaknesses) for senior high schools is to hold three banquets each year. They should be held within two weeks after the last event for that season and should include the junior varsity teams. The director of athletics should be responsible for these banquets.

The fall banquet would include the football and cross-country teams, and cheerleaders. Some schools also include the majorettes and marching band members.

The winter banquet should honor the basketball, wrestling, swimming, and gymnastics teams and cheerleaders.

The spring banquet would host the track, baseball, golf, and tennis teams.

It is highly recommended to have these banquets co-sponsored by the Booster Club of the school and by local service clubs. The board of education, administration, the team physician, local newspaper sports editor, the mayor of the city, and the recreation director should be included in the guest list.

If the school cafeteria is an adequate facility, this is the ideal place for these occasions.

The planning and preparation of these banquets requires considerable work and organization. The following checklist includes many of the items that require attention.

1. Date and place
2. Building permits
3. Printing of tickets
4. Meetings of Boosters Club representatives and service club representatives.
5. Program for banquet
6. Menu
7. Publicity (by all ground involved)

8. Distribution of tickets (to teams, to service clubs, to Boosters Club, to guests, etc.)
9. Squad lists and other information for program.
10. Printing of program
11. Information of program, etc. to coaches and administration
12. Team meeting
13. Guest list (send to master of ceremonies)
14. Reservations
15. Table decorations and favors
16. Order special awards
17. Public address system
18. Coat racks
19. Name cards for head table
20. Special seating arrangements
21. Pictures for papers
22. Thank you letters to master of ceremonies, service clubs, Booster Club, and others who took part in the program.

One of the most difficult decisions to make in planning any athletic banquet is to determine the best possible format. This sort of thing, like many others, tends to go in cycles. For example, should we have a speaker? If so, what background should he have? Can we limit him to twenty minutes? If he is near the end of the program, will he still command the interest of the people?

Other questions may include the kinds of awards given at banquets, the role of the master of ceremonies, the person selected for the invocation, etc.

The following suggested format may be helpful in planning athletic banquets:

DINNER–(If cafeteria style, have invocation following meal. If not, open with invocation.)

INVOCATION–By local clergyman or student member of Fellowship of Christian Athletes

15 MINUTE BREAK–For clearing of tables

MASTER OF CEREMONIES–Opening remarks

WELCOME TALKS–(2-3 minutes each) By presidents of service clubs sponsoring the banquet and president of the Boosters Club.

INTRODUCTION OF SPECIAL GUESTS

SPECIAL MUSIC–(If time permits)

SPEAKER–(If program is not too long otherwise.)

INTRODUCTION OF TEAMS AND REMARKS–By head coaches (include special awards.)

SENIOR RESPONSE–(By member of a team thanking sponsoring groups, coaches, parents, etc.)

SCHOOL SONG

FINAL REMARKS–(By Master of Ceremonies)

These banquets should start promptly at 6:30 p.m. or a comparable time and end by 9:00 p.m. The director of athletics should meet with the coaches and teams being honored approximately three weeks before the banquet. At that time complimentary tickets may be given to the players and a discussion may be held on items such as dress, attitude, manners, etc. as they pertain to the banquets.

Cafeteria style banquets or catered meals are most frequently used. Potluck dinners, especially when smaller numbered groups are honored, can be very popular.

Regular athletic banquets at the junior high schools should be discouraged. Pre-season programs followed by refreshments are very adequate. Some schools have potluck dinners at the junior high schools following the season. These can be worthwhile on an informal basis.

BASIC POLICY FOR ASSEMBLIES

Most of the basic policies and procedures regarding assemblies were discussed in Chapter 2. Several other items should also be stressed in this regard.

First, the assemblies should be scheduled sufficiently in advance so that they may be held at approximately the same dates as the banquets. The assemblies are more meaningful to the athletes if this can be done.

Second, regular athletic awards should be presented at the school assemblies. Trophies won by the teams should also be presented to the principal at these programs.

Third, this is the ideal time to give brief reviews of the seasons just completed and to thank the faculty and student body for their support.

Fourth, athletes should be properly dressed and seated in the front rows of the auditorium or on the stage if room permits. This saves considerable time in coming forward for their awards.

Assemblies should be well organized and planned to move quickly and efficiently. Pep assemblies are discussed in detail in Chapter 14.

INVOLVEMENT OF BOOSTERS CLUBS AND SERVICE CLUBS

The question as to what part a Boosters Club or service clubs may play in athletic banquets is frequently asked. Their involvement is important for many reasons.

In order to cover the details, the director of athletics should call a meeting of representatives of the various groups participating in these programs. The responsibilities of these clubs should be clearly spelled out.

The following details would normally be discussed:

First, the banquet program should be planned. Although the basic format might not change much from one banquet to another, each item should be thoroughly covered.

Second, the menu should be arranged. Different possibilities may also exist here. Since the students are being honored, their general likes and dislikes should be weighed.

Third, the guarantee of money by the clubs should be discussed. Since each coach and student will receive complimentary tickets, the problem of defraying the balance of the cost can be quite high.

Fourth, publicity in the papers and the bulletins released by the clubs taking part is important.

Fifth, the pre-sale of tickets to club members and the need for accurate reservations must also be stressed.

The director of athletics must also give recognition to these sponsoring clubs through the newspapers, during the banquet program, and by thank you letters following the banquets.

AWARD SYSTEM

The athletic awards system is different in nearly every school. The regular or traditional awards and special awards will vary considerably. The awards system should be included in the policies and procedures handbook used by the administration, coaches, and all others working in the athletic program.

The awards system should also be included in senior high school and junior high school student handbooks. Special citizenship, memorial, or scholar-athlete awards pertaining to that particular sport are desirable. Service bars may also be used.

The director of athletics and coaches must carefully guard against excessive "gingerbread" on letter sweaters by certain groups or individuals. This can cheapen or distract from an otherwise attractive award.

In sports such as football and basketball the athletic council will require an athlete to participate in a certain number of quarters. This usually means about half of the quarters. Seniors in any sport who have not accumulated sufficient points for an award may be given one upon the coach's recommendation. This is true if he has been a team member for at least one other year and did not receive an award before his senior year.

The question of giving awards to injured players who have not received sufficient points is sometimes difficult to resolve: Seniors should be given special consideration in these cases.

Any awards system requires periodic study and revision. New coaches bring new ideas which may help update these policies.

Wrestling awards, for example, were frequently based on the number of wins or points scored by an individual. A boy could conceivably wrestle in every scheduled match and not letter because of his win-loss record. This is not the policy in team sports such as football, basketball, baseball, etc. Should this be the case in wrestling?

Swimming and track awards are still based largely on points scored by individuals or relay teams. These standards must be realistic so that a reasonable number of boys will letter. The system for granting letters in swimming for the Berea City Schools is based on 50 points including 10 points for training. Deductions for unexcused absence from practice will result in forfeiting an award. The balance of the swimming award policy is:

Winning an event in a dual meet ---------------------- 5 points
2nd place in an event in a dual meet ------------------- 3 points
3rd place in an event in a dual meet -------------------- 1 point

Winning relay in a dual meet (each boy) ---------------- 5 points
Winning an event in a district meet ---------------------10 points
2nd place in a district meet ---------------------------- 8 points
3rd place in an event in a district meet ------------------ 6 points
4th place in an event in a district meet ------------------ 4 points
5th place in an event in a district meet ------------------ 2 points

In Relay Meet Events

1st place–each boy ----------------- 5 points
2nd place–each boy ----------------- 4 points
3rd place–each boy ----------------- 3 points
4th place–each boy ----------------- 2 points
5th place–each boy ----------------- 1 point

Junior varsity boys who swim in a varsity event will be awarded all training and attendance points for the year, in addition to points earned in the varsity event.

In State High School meet–double the district meet points. A boy who earns an average of three points for half of the dual meets and cannot participate further because of injury may be awarded a letter upon recommendation of the coach.

A definite policy for managers, assistant manager, scorekeepers, statisticians, and trainers must be included. If junior varsity awards are presented this policy must be clearly spelled out. Certificates and numerals rather than smaller or special letters for junior varsity teams prove quite satisfactory.

Junior high school awards policies should be based on the number of games played in their schedules. These policies will be somewhat similar to the varsity system.

Most senior and junior high schools have special awards presented at the end of the season or at the end of the school year. Care must be taken not to include too many of these honors or there will be a tendency for all of them to lose their importance.

Babe Ruth Sportsmanship Awards, Memorial Awards honoring deceased coaches or athletes, and Scholar-Athlete awards are most significant.

One of the newer awards of this type is the National Scholar-Athlete Award Program co-sponsored by the National Council of State High School Coaches Associations, American Association for Health, Physical Education, and Recreation, and the National Association of Secondary School Principals. This program has been developed for the purpose of giving recognition to high school athletes who excel not only in sports but also in academic pursuits, leadership, and citizenship. All boys in high school (grades 9-12) who have a cumulative grade average of "B" or 85 percent, or the equivalent in the grading system for that particular school, have received a varsity letter for participation on any sports team sponsored by the school, and have demonstrated exemplary citizenship and personal qualities, are eligible to receive a beautifully designed award certificate.

This award has also been sanctioned and promoted by the National Council of Secondary School Athletic Directors.

Guidelines should be used for determining recipients of special awards. This is most beneficial to the committee in making the final selection.

Each year the Babe Ruth Sportsmanship Award is presented to a senior boy at the senior high schools in the Berea City School District. The head coaches each nominate one boy for consideration. After all of the nominations are received by the director of athletics, a ballot is prepared. A sample is shown in Figure 12-1.

The voting is done by the principal, director of athletics, faculty manager, and head coaches. The recipient is given a special medal and his name is engraved on a plaque retained in the school trophy case. A similar award is given to a senior girl each year.

GENERAL PROGRAM FOR GIRLS' INTERSCHOLASTIC ATHLETICS

The girls' interscholastic athletics program is really on the move. It is one that we no longer can ignore and must be prepared to implement if we have not done so already.

Mr. John K. Cotton, Director of Athletics and Physical Education, Farmington Public Schools, Farmington, Michigan has an excellent article dealing with girls' athletics in a recent issue of "The Athletic Director." This is a newsletter published five times each year by the National Council of Secondary School Athletic Directors, a council of the Division of Men's Athletics of the American Association for Health, Physical Education, and Recreation.

The following portion of Mr. Cotton's article sets a good tone for establishing a sound girls' athletics program:

Through the media of our newly formed National Council of Secondary School Athletic Directors I take a stand for girls'

Berea City Schools

Berea, Ohio 44017

THE BABE RUTH SPORTSMANSHIP AWARD

School year 19x5–19x6

Midpark High School

The following boys have been nominated by the head coaches. Please rate these boys from 1, 2, 3, 4,–No. 1 being your first choice.

Consider sportsmanship in its widest educational aspect–in the schoolroom, on the athletic field and playground, in the home, at the church, and as part of the local community. All awards are for sportsmanship–not competitive excellence, popularity, number of athletic letters, and such, except when they indicate achievement in the broader sense.

Bill Baker	
Jack Jones	
Fred Miller	
Tim Smith	

Please return to me as soon as possible.

Bob Purdy
Athletic Director

Figure 12-1

athletic programs. It is my contention that the board of education, superintendent, principal, athletic director, or coach who offers resistance to an orderly expansion of girls' athletics is wrong and knows he is wrong. I don't believe we can in all honesty say "go slow," using this term as a crutch, while attempting to rationalize the aborting of girls' programs.

The implementation of a girls' sports program requires a great deal of unity, empathy, and understanding between involved personnel. Our hang-up is analogous to that of some of the peace talks–plenty of discussion but little or no concrete or definitive action for negotiating a peace settlement. In girls' athletics, we continue to discuss the problems related to the program while the girls, with no athletics, remain the losers.

I would suggest action rather than dialogue. The person who reads this journal is well versed in the so-called problems of girls' athletics. At this point and time we should not look back and make an in-depth study of the past. Rather, let's look to the future and realistically appraise the task of the athletic director who should play a major role in leadership. The challenge of the seventies in our profession is to get off dead center in girls' sports. If you offer nothing for girls–you should get started. If you offer a token–you have an obligation to expand these offerings. Incidentally, let's call a spade a spade: *Girls' Athletics.* Not play days–not sport days–not extended programs for girls–not extramurals, but well rounded interscholastic athletics.

I believe that the objectives and desirable outcomes of competitive programs for girls should be similar to boys but should not emulate boys' programs. Making comparisons between boys' and girls' athletics can be odious. It is important to note that girls' athletics should not be restricted because future opportunities for girls in athletics are not the same as for boys; or because the prestige syndrome is different; or because of the femininity hang-up.

Pressures which once suggested that girls are unable to compete have been removed. There is no research that suggests girls can be harmed by competition. It has been said by many proponents of girls' athletics that they can be injured, they can be emotionally upset, they can be exhausted–but so can boys!

The sympathetic athletic director must take the leadership in the mechanical implementation of girls' athletics. He should schedule, contract, budget, hire officials, etc., much in the same way as he does for boys. But he should be delicate in not striving for control–his goal should be leadership and support. He should counsel the women coaches in developing girls athletics as an educational tool, in establishing a philosophy toward winning and losing, and in determining what school policy will be developed relative to gate receipts.

Before the formation of a girls' interscholastic athletic conference, certain organizational guidelines and other conditions must be agreed upon. When the Girls' Interscholastic League involving Parma, Normandy and Valley Forge High Schools of the Parma City Schools, Berea and Midpark High Schools of the Berea City Schools, and Strongsville High School was formed, the following guidelines, conditions, policies, and principles were adopted.

PROPOSED ORGANIZATIONAL GUIDELINES:

1. Each school will play the other schools involved only once.
2. The winner should be determined by the win-loss record.
3. A. Bad weather is the only excuse for game cancellation without penalty. If this situation arises, the game should be rescheduled at a later date agreeable to both schools.
   B. If game is cancelled due to lack of transportation or limited facilities, it is a forfeit and not to be rescheduled.
4. Officials are to be drawn from a predetermined list agreed upon by all the coaches.
5. A social hour following the game is to be provided by the host school.
6. Scholastic records of the participants should be submitted to the athletic director who in turn will submit it to the state.
7. Game contracts and/or master schedules should be negotiated on approved state association forms or similar copy.
8. Each participant should have insurance and is responsible for any and all medical expenses as a result of this program. Parents should provide information on current insurance which is primary coverage.
9. A secretary should be selected for the purpose of collecting game results to all coaches of the schools involved.

She will also be responsible for tabulating the win-loss records of the schools involved. The winning coach is responsible for phoning in the results of the contest within forty-eight hours after it has taken place.

10. Each participant must have a medical examination by the school doctor or through their personal physician.
11. All DGWS and OHSAA rules and regulations governing girl's interscholastics must be followed.
12. Sport Season Calendar:
    Volleyball–October, November, early December
    Basketball–January, February, March
    Softball–April, May

AGREEMENT CONDITIONS PERTAINING TO THE PROPOSED GIRLS' INTERSCHOLASTIC LEAGUE

1. This arrangement is to be conducted on a trial basis and there will be no binding contract or constitution prohibiting a school to withdraw from this association if they so desire.
2. During the trial period, this association of schools shall not be designated as a league.
3. Competitive levels among the schools are to be relatively equal to insure a beneficial learning experience for the students.
4. All sports shall be taught and coached by qualified faculty women.
5. Adequate, DGWS approved facilities and equipment should be available several times a week immediately after school for the purpose of scheduled practiced and/or games in order that the personal safety of the participants need not be jeopardized.
6. The purpose of games should be for the participants to experience a high level of competition and an atmosphere of fellowship and sportsmanship.
7. There are to be no presentations of awards of monetary value.
8. The final scheduling of games is to be determined and agreed upon by all coaches concerned before September 30 each year.

9. Games with schools outside this association can be scheduled in addition to the contests scheduled with the above mentioned schools.

POLICIES AND PRINCIPLES GOVERNING THE ADMINISTRATION OF GIRLS' INTERSCHOLASTIC ATHLETICS

Competitive sports are an inherent part of the total physical education program for girls in secondary schools. When properly organized and conducted, inter-school athletics provide numerous opportunities for girls to participate in activities which promote growth and development, teach social and recreational skills, and develop leadership qualities. These values are more readily attained when the program is based upon accepted standards and practices developed by professional leaders in physical education and athletics and when competing teams are members of and follow the rules and regulations approved by a state high school athletic association. These rules and regulations for Girls' Interscholastic Athletics of the Ohio High School Athletic Association are based upon the following principles and policies:

1. The major emphasis on girls' interscholastic athletics should be upon skilled play and good sportsmanship. Competition would be equitable in order that full learning and enjoyment may be realized from game participation.
2. Every attempt should be made to provide favorable playing conditions in order that the competitive experiences of the girls may be wholesome and result in the attainment of desirable attitudes and conduct.
3. The interscholastic program should be a direct outgrowth of the broad instructional and intramural programs and should include a wide variety of activities.
4. The program should be financed by budget organizational and school funds rather than by admission charges.
5. The rules, regulations and supervision of the program should insure the maximum protection of the health and safety of the players.
6. Limitations should be placed upon the length of the sport season, the number of practice periods and the number of interscholastic contests played.

7. It is recommended that a girl be a member of no more than one interscholastic team at any one time.
8. Competitive events for girls should be arranged separately from competitive events for boys except in the approved co-recreational activities. Girls' events should be played according to current DGWS rules with qualified persons officiating.
9. The school administrator is responsible for the administration and supervision of the girls' interscholastic athletic program.
10. The home team should make a determined effort to have some social activity for the competitors in connection with the interscholastic event.

RULES COVERAGE AND REGULATIONS FOR CONTESTS

The Ohio High School Athletic Association has adopted the following rules and regulations for the Girls' Interscholastic Athletic program. Unless otherwise specified the rules pertaining to the boys program shall also apply to the girls.

Girls' Rules and Regulations

RULE 1–APPROVED RULES

Section 1. officials rules

In girls' interscholastic sports events, current rules of the Division for Girls' and Women's Sports of the American Association for Health, Physical Education and Recreation must be used. Rules for sports not covered by the DGWS must be those approved by the OHSAA .

RULE 2–RULE COVERAGE

Section 1. grade level

Girls enrolled in grades nine, ten, eleven and twelve in high schools belonging to the Association may participate in the approved interscholastic program.

Section 2. sponsorship

All games, previews and other athletic contests involving member schools must be under the direct sponsorship and supervision of the schools themselves. This included A.A.U. and similar meets except that high school meets sponsored and supervised by approved colleges and universities may be sanctioned by applying to the office of the OHSAA for consideration of approval.

Section 3. playing on independent teams

After a pupil has become a member of a high school squad, she shall not take part in a contest on an independent team in the same sport until her squad has closed its season for that sport. A pupil is a member of a squad when she participates in a game or meet.

Section 4. girls' sports participation card

Schools must designate sponsored girls' interscholastic sports on the Girls' Official Sports Participation Card to be filed in the OHSAA office by October 1.

Section 5. no curtain raisers

Interscholastic games or meets between girls' teams shall not be played as preliminaries, curtain raisers, double headers, or at any other time in connection with boys' events.

Section 6. no competition against boys

Girls' teams shall not compete interscholastically against a boys team.

Section 7. girls only

Girls' teams must be composed of girls only for interscholastic contests.

Section 8. scrimmage and practice limitations

Contests and scrimmages with college level teams and organized adult independent teams are prohibited.

Section 9. no football type games

The State Board of Control does not approve football type games (flag, touch, tag, powder puff, etc.) as part of the girls' interscholastic program.

RULE 3–FINANCES

Section 1. financing

It is recommended that financing of girls' interscholastic program be included in the total school budget or other school approved organizational funds.

Section 2. paid admissions

Paid admissions for girls' interscholastic contests shall be the prerogative of the sponsoring school.

RULE 4–APPROVAL OF CONTESTS AND TRAVEL

Section 1. administrative responsibilities

All girls' interscholastic games shall be approved by the school administration and when travel is involved, the form of transportation shall be approved by the school administration.

Section 2. game contracts

Game contracts for girls' interscholastic contests must be negotiated on approved OHSAA forms.

Section 3. contests with non-member schools

The consent of the Commissioner must be secured before engaging in contests with schools that are not members of the Association.

RULE 5–CO-EDUCATIONAL ACTIVITIES

Schools may be represented by boys and girls in the following mixed events–

> Archery, Badminton, Bowling, Deck Tennis, Golf, Horseshoe Pitching, Riflery, Shuffleboard, Skating, Table Tennis, Tennis and Volleyball

Participants cannot be members of the interscholastic squads.

RULE 6–CERTIFICATED TEACHERS

All coaches shall be certificated teachers locally employed by the Board of Education and their entire salary shall be paid by that body. All sports shall be taught and coached by qualified faculty women whenever and wherever possible.

RULE 7–FACULTY REPRESENTATIVE

A woman faculty member shall supervise and accompany the school group at all contests.

RULE 8–OFFICIALS

DGWS approved, rated officials must be used in all girls' interscholastic athletic contests whenever and wherever possible.

RULE 9–RECOGNIZED SPORTS

Section 1. competition

A high school girl may participate in the following: archery, badminton, basketball, bowling, fencing, field hockey, golf, gymnastics, softball, soccer, swimming, track and field, tennis and volleyball. (Fall, Winter, Spring).

Section 2. contests in the association's non-recognized sports

Names of members of teams in sports not recognized by the State Association but sponsored by a league or school system must be listed on the Official Ohio High School Athletic Association eligibility blanks and all State Association rules are to apply.

Section 3. track and field

Boys' and girls' track meets may take place simultaneously. There must be at least four (4) track and field events scheduled for girls in such a meet.

Section 4. gymnastics

Boys' and girls' gymnastic meets may take place simultaneously. There must be at least two (2) events scheduled for girls in such a meet.

Section 5. swimming

Boys' and girls' swimming meets may take place simultaneously. There must be at least four (4) events scheduled for girls in such a meet.

RULE 10–ATHLETIC PARTICIPATION FORMS REQUIRED

Athletic participation forms, properly signed by a physician, by the participant and by one of her parents or guardians must be on file with the Administrator before any candidate for a team may participate in a practice. These forms necessitate the physician's certification of the individual's physical fitness no less than once each school year.

RULE 11–CHARACTER OR CONDUCT

In matters pertaining to personal conduct in which athletics are not involved, the school itself is to be the sole judge as to whether the pupil may play on its teams.

In matters pertaining to personal conduct in which athletics are involved, such as gross violations of sportsmanship, attacks on officials, etc., the State Association shall have jurisdiction to determine the penalties involved and whether or not the pupil may participate in athletics.

RULE 12–SCHOLARSHIP

To be eligible during any semester, a girl must have passed during the immediately preceding semester in subjects which count one and one-half units per semester toward graduation. (Boys Rule 7, "Scholarship" applies.)

RULE 13–ELIGIBILITY LIST

The administrative head of the school is required to have available on request a list of the names of the girls eligible for each sport season.

RULE 14–INTERSCHOLASTIC COMPETITION

Interscholastic competition is sports competition in which the participants from each school compete as a team. This includes scheduled contests, sports day, telegraphic meets, invitational meets, alumni games, interschool scrimmages and exhibitions.

Exceptions: Instructional clinics designed for the teaching of fundamental skills and conducted for learning theory, techniques, rules, game procedure, strategy, etc. shall not be counted as a scheduled contest. Such clinics must be conducted by authorized groups.

RULE 15–LIMIT OF PARTICIPATION

Section 1. number of contests

A high school girl may play in twelve (12) interscholastic contests per sport per school year in school sponsored girls' interscholastic activities.

Section 2. contests per day

A girl may play in one (1) contest per day in any sport as approved by Rule 9.

There shall be no more than two (2) contests per week, which are not to be played on consecutive days.

Exceptions: Sports Days. Section 2 does not apply when Sports Days are conducted on a non-school day. Participation must involve three or more schools. ALL GAMES PLAYED WILL COUNT ON TOTAL GAME LIMITATION.

RULE 16–ATHLETIC AWARDS

Approved athletic awards which may be accepted by the pupil from any source consist of those usually given, such as letters, ribbons, scrolls, banners, medals, charms, gold basketballs, baseballs, track insignia, lapel pins, plaques, cups, trophies, and college scholarships, provided the amount of the scholarship is paid directly to the college of choice by the donors.

Awards from any source which will not be approved by the Association for participation in interscholastic athletics consist of sweaters, jerseys, blazers, jackets, any other type of wearing apparel or any award exceeding one dollar ($1.00) in value other than those listed in the preceding paragraph.

A sweater, jacket, or jersey accepted by a high school pupil for playing on an amateur, non-school sponsored team is not to be considered a violation of this rule.

The school itself must be held accountable to the Association for any violation of this rule, even by individuals or groups before, at, or after graduation

RULE 17—VIOLATION OF RULES

Section 1. protests

Fairness and courtesy demand that rumors and factors relative to a violation of these rules and regulations be presented at the earliest possible date to the principal for investigation. A written report or request for investigation must be filed with the Commissioner.

Section 2. penalties

Penalties assessed by the Commissioner or by the Board of Control upon member schools for violation of these rules will vary from a warning through probation to suspension depending upon the character of the violation.

RULE 18—REGULATIONS

The board of control may make regulations and interpretations to promote the aims and interests of this Association in accordance with the foregoing general regulations for girls' interscholastic sports.

THIRTEEN

Implementing Advantageous Insurance and Medical Assistance for the Athletic Program

The purpose of this chapter is to discuss the implementation of advantageous insurance protection and the proper medical assistance necessary in conducting athletic programs.

There are many types of insurance needed. In fact there are many different types of accident insurance plans alone, to say nothing of the policies to cover coaches on the job, fidelity bonds, theft insurance, fire insurance, etc. The portion of this chapter devoted to insurance will deal with athletic accident insurance.

SCHOOL INSURANCE PLAN

Although most school systems do not feel that they are in the insurance business per se, there is a definite obligation to have specific policies and procedures pertaining to athletic accident insurance. These policies should be a part of the regular operating code of the athletic department. All administrators, faculty managers, and coaches must be well aware of these policies. In turn, the players and their parents must also be advised as to these procedures.

It is necessary to have every athlete competing in any phase of the program to be properly covered by insurance before he is permitted to practice or compete.

Programs involving insurance protection differ greatly with school systems even within close proximity of others. Much depends on what has been done before, the money available for such protection, and the plans offered by the state athletic associations.

The Berea City School District in Ohio has employed the following program in recent years. A very large and prominent insurance company has made available student accident insurance policies for a very nominal figure. These policies cover all injuries sustained in practice sessions and in games, travel to and from games, etc. All sports at all levels but high school football are included in this plan.

Parents of students participating in high school football are advised by letter that the family hospitalization plan and/or a football accident insurance plan are necessary before any boy may compete or practice. These are the responsibility of the parents to be certain that their sons are properly covered. The head football coaches also keep records of the type of family insurance, the policy number, and other important information.

The letter in Figure 13-1 is sent to each head football coach at the high school level in early August.

The head coach in turn writes each parent explaining the school's policy regarding football coverage. This letter is mailed in conjunction with training rules for the athletes as they pertain to the approaching season.

If athletes are not covered by family hospitalization plans and are unable financially to purchase the football accident insurance policy, the school athletic department will pay these premiums.

In all other sports on all levels, each athlete must have hospitalization coverage through the family or be protected by the regular school insurance program. The parents of these athletes should also be advised by letter concerning this policy.

Occasionally parents are unwilling to enroll their children in the school insurance program, even though their family hospitalization may not completely cover all aspects necessary. The athletes should not be allowed to practice or compete until a letter is on file from the parent to the effect that they will assume the full

Date

To: Coaches of Varsity and Junior Varsity Interschool Football Teams, Grades 10, 11, and 12:

Boys participating in the high school (grades 10, 11, 12) Varsity Football program will be offered a plan of accident insurance protection to cover injuries they might receive while practicing for or playing in such games, or while traveling directly to or from such practice or games. Benefits are payable in addition to any other insurance benefits the player may receive as a result of the same injury. Cost to the player is $10.00 for the try-out player August 15 to September 15, and $20.00 for the team player September 15 to December 15.

Materials relative to this insurance are enclosed for your information. It should be noted that this plan is unusual in that it provides coverage for eye and tooth damage, and that benefits are payable whether the insured is treated in the hospital emergency room, as a hospital inpatient, or in the doctor's office.

You will be especially interested in the fact that you, as a member of the coaching staff, have already been enrolled for this insurance protection. Your insurance identification card is enclosed. There is no charge to you for this protection. Please notice that the policy applies only to accidents connected with your interschool football coaching activities with players in grades 10, 11, and 12.

If you have questions about the plan, please contact me.

Robert Purdy
Director of Athletics

Figure 13-1

responsibility for all hospital and medical bills not covered by the family hospitalization.

STATE APPROVED ACTIVITY ACCIDENT PLAN

The Ohio High School Athletic Association, in October of 1970, approved the offering of a voluntary Student Accident Insurance Plan to supplement the already existing state association catastrophe plan. This program was installed in Ohio on a pilot project basis in 1970-1971. This same program has been successful in other states having a state sponsored catastrophic plan similar to that of Ohio.

The basic plan is as follows:

Description of $5,000 Activity Accident Insurance Plan Approved by the OHSAA

PURPOSE:

1. The plan provides insurance for the student who either does not have insurance, or whose family insurance will only pay for part of the expenses.
2. The cost of the plan is low, largely because the amount of any collectible insurance is deducted from the amount otherwise payable on account of a claim.

WHY PLAN IS NEEDED:

With the ever increasing hospital and doctor bills, it is becoming more difficult to provide a means to meet medical needs so it will not be a financial burden on a family if one of their members become involved in an accident going to, from, or at school. The OHSAA plan could be the vital link for a family in case of costly doctor and hospital bills.

WHICH SCHOOLS ARE ELIGIBLE:

Each school which is a member of the OHSAA is eligible.

WHO IS COVERED:

Thee OHSAA plan covers *all* students in *any* school activity. A student is insured when:

(1) Attending or performing his assigned duties while on the school premises during school hours, including supervised lunch hours, and recesses, or the days when the student has scheduled classes; or

(2) Attending or participating in activities sponsored by the school, during or after school hours, provided the particular activity is directly supervised by the school through an employee thereof designated by the school for that purpose who is present at such activity; or

(3) Practicing for or competing in, as a representative of the member school and under direct supervision of a full-time school employee, an inter-school activity conducted under the regulation and jurisdiction of the Ohio High School Athletic Association; or

(4) Traveling directly to or from such practice or competition (1) in a school bus operated by a properly licensed driver, or (2) in a private vehicle designated by and under the direct supervision of the school and operated by a properly licensed adult driver.

BENEFITS OF THE PLAN

Benefits are payable up to a maximum of $5,000, subject to a deductible equal to all other benefits paid or collectible on account of the same injury.

Benefits will be paid on the basis of reasonable and customary expenses incurred within one year from the date of injury. The reasonable expense for hospital room and board will be the usual charge by the hospital for semi-private room, and the reasonable expense of dental treatment shall not exceed $100 per damaged tooth.

SCHOOL OFFICIALS COOPERATION

The premiums for this plan are lower than many schools now pay for football coverages alone. This is possible only because other collectible insurance is taken into account in calculating the amount the insurance company has to pay. In effect, this means that the other collectible insurance deductible operates so that the family of the injured student does not make a profit. Many families object strongly to the operation of other collectible insurance features, and in many instances complain to school officials.

It has been established that a careful explanation as to the effect the other insurance deductible feature has on claims, and in turn on cost, will frequently soothe the feelings of the complaining parent. The cooperation of school officials in this connection is urgently required. The insurance company will make every effort to uncover other collectible insurance with respect to each claim. Through the mutual cooperation of school officials and the company, it is hoped that the plan will work to the satisfaction of all concerned.

CATASTROPHIC INSURANCE

A number of school systems in the United States had paid catastrophic insurance policies to cover athletes for serious injuries involving unusually large hospital and medical expenses. In the past few years the trend has been toward the state athletic association to provide for this coverage.

This plan enables all students engaged in a school sanctioned athletic activity of which they are a member to be included in this policy.

The Ohio High School Athletic Association has adopted the policy shown in Figure 13-2 for all of its member schools both at the junior and senior high school levels. This service is rendered at no cost to any school or individual, but is paid for entirely by the state association.

Description of Catastrophic Injury Policy
insuring students of member schools
of
Ohio High School Athletic Association
(hereinafter called the Association)

Students of schools which are members of the above Association are insured, in accordance with the provisions of the Catastrophic Injury Policy issued to the Association, against loss caused solely by accidental bodily injury, incurred while the policy is in force and while –

(a) practicing for or competing in, as a representative of the member school and under direct supervision of a full-time school employee, an inter-school activity conducted under the regulation and jurisdiction of the above Association, or

(b) traveling, in a group of two or more, directly to or from such practice or competition (1) in a school bus operated by a properly licensed driver or (2) in a private vehicle designated by and under the direct supervision of the school and operated by a properly licensed adult driver.

The benefits of the policy are shown in Figure 13-2. All benefits are covered by and subject in every respect to the Catastrophic Injury Policy, which alone constitutes the agreement under which payments are made.

NOTICE OF INJURY MUST BE GIVEN TO THE COMPANY WITHIN THIRTY DAYS FOLLOWING DATE OF INJURY AND A COMPLETED

Figure 13-2

CLAIM FORM MUST BE FURNISHED TO THE COMPANY WITHIN NINETY DAYS AFTER THE DATE OF INJURY.

MEDICAL–DENTAL–HOSPITAL EXPENSE

Part A:

If injury covered by this policy requires treatment within thirty days after the date of injury by a licensed Doctor of Medicine, Osteopathy or Dentistry, or confinement in a licensed hospital, the Company will pay the reasonable and customary expenses incurred for necessary medical, dental and hospital care within one year from the date of injury up to a maximum of $100,000 for any one injury, which are in excess of the deductible amount.
The reasonable and customary expense

(a) For hospital room and board shall be the hospital's most common charge for its semi-private room accommodations; and

(b) For dental treatment shall not exceed $100 per damaged tooth.

The deductible amount referred to above shall be the greater of

(a) $5,000 or

(b) the total benefits payable for the same loss, on a provision of service basis or on an expense incurred basis under any other collectible policy or service contract where such other policy or service contract has been in effect longer than coverage under this policy, unless otherwise herein provided.

DEATH, DISMEMBERMENT, AND LOSS OF SIGHT:

Part B:

If injury covered by this policy does, within 120 days from date of injury, result directly and independently of all other causes in any of the specific losses enumerated in this Part B, the Company will pay indemnity in the amount set opposite such loss, but only one of the amounts, the largest so specified, which is applicable to a loss sustained, will be paid for injuries to any one insured. Loss of hand or foot means loss by severance at or above the wrist or ankle joint. Loss of sight must be entire and irrecoverable. Any indemnity payable under Part B will be in addition to any indemnity otherwise payable under this policy.

Loss of Life	$1,000
Loss of Both Hands, Both Feet, or Sight of Both Eyes	$1,000
Loss of One Hand, One Foot, or Sight of One Eye	$ 500

EXCLUSIONS:

Part C:

No benefits shall be payable

(a) for or on account of treatment of hernia, appendicitis, cardiac disease, diabetes, detached retina, osteomyelitis, malignancy or Osgood-Schlatter's Disease; or

(b) for aggravation of a pre-existing condition; or

(c) for physical therapy or drugs, except while hospital confined; or

(d) for injuries connected with fighting or brawling or self-inflicted injuries; or

(e) for secondary infections.

POLICY ON HANDLING ATHLETIC INJURIES

Every athletic department should have a clearly defined policy for dealing with athletic injuries. The coaches should be trained in basic first aid procedures for "on the spot" treatment. The more serious injuries would involve proper care and attention to the athlete pending the arrival of an ambulance or fire department rescue squad.

A coach should accompany any athlete being taken to the hospital or doctor's office. He should remain until the parents arrive and assume the responsibility and he is no longer needed. Team trainers and team physicians can assume an important role in this regard during games and practice sessions.

Parents should be notified immediately of their son's or daughter's injury and advised as to what has been done and the hospital or doctor's office to which they were taken.

The head coach, trainer, and team physician should follow closely the progress of these cases. No athlete who has sustained a serious injury should be allowed to return to practice or competition without the approval of the physician in charge. Recommended plans for gradually returning these athletes to top physical condition should be carefully followed.

The Berea City School District requires the use of a school injury report form. This is made of in duplicate by the person reporting the injury with the building principal and supervisor of special services receiving copies.

A sample of this report form is shown in Figure 13-3.

PHYSICAL EXAMINATIONS

No athlete should be allowed to practice or compete on any squad without first having a physical examination by a physician. These are usually conducted at the school clinic with nurses assisting the physicians with certain phases of the examination. Athletes who missed these examinations at the school must go to

BEREA CITY SCHOOL DISTRICT
BEREA, OHIO 44017

SCHOOL INJURY REPORT

Date____________________

Name____________________ Building____________________

Student____________________ Employee____________________

Date of Injury____________________ Hour________A.M.____P.M.____

In the space below, describe where (hall, playground, etc.) and how (fall, collision, etc.) the injury occurred:

____

____

____

In the space below, describe the nature of the injury and the part of the body that was affected:

____

____

____

What first aid was given?______________________________

____

Final disposition (Clinic, Parents Called, Hospital, etc.)):____________________

____

Who witnessed the injury?______________________________

Person Reporting:______________________________

Principal's Signature______________________________

If an employee, will a workman's compensation form be completed? Yes____

No____

Please provide this essential information in duplicate. One will be filed by the principal. The other will go to the Supervisor of Special Services.

Figure 13-3

another school in the system on the day they are scheduled or must see their family physician. The regular card approved by the state athletic association should be properly filled in and signed by the physician. A sample of the cards used in the state of Ohio by member schools of the state athletic association is shown in Chapter 8.

The director of athletics and the school nurses should work closely in scheduling these physical examinations. This is most important, so that the physicians, coaches, and athletes have sufficient notice and can plan accordingly.

Each athlete should be examined at least once per school year. If he is badly injured during a particular season, he should be examined again before the start of another season.

Dr. H. Roger Collins, an orthopedic surgeon with the Cleveland Clinic Foundation, has specialized with sports medicine for a number of years. He presented some excellent views on the role of physicians as they pertain to the importance of the physical examination at a recent meeting of the Cuyahoga County School Health Council. These views follow:

> The pre-participation physical examination serves three distinct functions: (1) It determines which athlete is physically qualified to participate in a given sport and eliminates the unfit. (2) It qualifies him as to the type of sport in which he may safely participate. (3) Treatment can be instituted to bring him to a physical level which will permit participation in a given sport and/or improve performance. For this reason, the exam should be held in May or June so that treatment and rehabilitation can be carried out over the summer.
>
> It has been shown that the best and most complete examinations are the result of the combined effort of the family physician and a special examination group. The family physician should be relied upon for information that might have a bearing as to the physical fitness of the youth. Immunizations, urinalysis, and a blood count should be included and sent to the school physician in writing. The examination by the school physician, or physicians, should be complete and thorough.
>
> Necessarily, this is designed as a screening procedure to eliminate the obviously unfit and segregate those with questionable defects for further definitive medical studies. Successive exams through the growing years are worthwhile. Many develop fitness for participation with physical maturity and physical eaucation. On initial examination the athlete should be classified as to body build, strength, and physical maturity, and care be taken to match him in order to prevent injuries.
>
> No game should begin until a physician is present. The physician can contribute much in providing medical and health bases for policies related to many aspects of the program (matching of players, length and frequency of contests and practice sessions, length of season, time of day for events, health matters related to travel, equipment and clothing, etc.)

THE FIELD OF SPORTS MEDICINE

The field of sports medicine is one of major significance in safeguarding the health of every young athlete.

Dr. Thomas E. Shaffer of the Department of Pediatrics, College of Medicine at Ohio State University has done much work in the area of sports medicine as a member of the Joint Committee on Physical Fitness, Recreation and Sports Medicine and the American Academy of Pediatrics. In a paper given at the Midwest States Regional Conference for Secondary School Athletic Directors in Indianapolis, Indiana on February 2, 1971, he presented several important issues concerning this topic:

> The critical issue is that of safeguarding the health of the young athlete. This subject is closely related to the broader problem of availability and use of health services in our country in this era when we know more about what can be done than we are actually doing. Most health programs for athlete are focused on prevention of accidents and injuries because physical activities signify an increased risk. The health professions have been slow to pick up on the total aspect of prevention, diagnosis, and treatment of sports-related health problems and it is common to find health program for athletes that are not as comprehensive or as available as would be desirable. We have an obligation to marshal the knowledge and understanding of the various professions who deal with young people toward a cooperative program in high schools which will equal the care and attention the superstars on professional and university teams receive. Sports medicine is a medical field of greater scope than the prevention and management of injuries. It applies to athletes of all levels–from the highly trained ones to the little leaguers, extends from research in physiology, psychology, and pathology to actual practice, and to be effective it will involve the great reservoir of professionals from the health specialties, education, athletic trainers, coaches, parents, and the competitors themselves. It is easy to express this concept, but not easy to accomplish it because concerted cooperative action is usually more difficult to accomplish than to "do it yourself."

Other thought-provoking ideas dealt with by Dr. Shaffer included:

1. The field of sports medicine cannot limit itself solely to prevention and management of injuries. Steps must be

taken to involve all levels of athletic participation, extend from research to actual practice situations, and to involve players, coaches, trainers, medical professionals and health and physical education specialists in preparing proper procedures in sports medicine.

2. Medical care programs cannot be planned only for the football type injury but must provide coverage and service for participants in all sports, girls as well as boys.
3. The concept of the Local Sports Medicine Council and its endorsement by the American Academy of Pediatrics is most noteworthy. This Council would have as its prime functions to:
   a. Study those local resources that are available for providing medical care for the athlete.
   b. Assist those national organizations which are recognized as leaders in health concerns of the athlete.
   c. Periodically study and evaluate equipment and maintenance of facilities.
   d. Analyze injury and sports related illnesses for the purpose of taking steps to eliminate recurrences.
   e. Assist in distribution of information pertaining to sports medicine to the proper community and school personnel.
   f. Promote in-service training workshops and conferences to improve competencies of those people involved in medical care of the athlete.
   g. Membership in the local sports medicine council should include: coach, trainer, physician, athlete, and school administrator.
4. In addition to the local sports medicine council, the American Medical Association (June, 1969) further encourages the development of the athletic medicine unit for every school that conducts an athletic program.

   This athletic medicine unit should be composed of a physician, a trainer and other necessary school personnel such as coach, school nurse and athletic director. The functions of the unit would be prevention of injury, provision of medical care in cooperation with the team doctor and family physician, assistance in rehabilitation of the injured, preparation of injury reports, and development of in-service training programs for all members of the athletic medicine unit and other related personnel.

5. Finally, Dr. Shaffer advocates a "Bill of Rights for the Athlete" that would safeguard the health and safety of the athlete. This Bill of Rights would include:

   a. Proper Equipment and Facilities
   Equipment must be properly fitted, kept clean and repaired after each season. Facilities must be kept in safe playing condition.

   b. Qualified Coaching
   The coach must have professional training in prevention and care of athletic injuries, especially so as it pertains to the particular sport(s) that he coaches. The coach must also keep records of injuries and actively participate in the athletic medicine unit.

   c. Good Officiating
   Officials must be able to recognize injuries, undue fatigue, etc., if the player is to be protected. Naturally, their application of the rules of the game will aid greatly in prevention of injuries.

   d. Sufficient and Proper Conditioning
   Conditioning programs must be designed to prepare the athlete for the particular sport as well as for return to participation after absence due to injury or illness.

   e. Medical Supervision and Care
   Thorough, complete physical examination of the athlete must be conducted at least once a year.
   The services of a team physician must be available to assist in such matters as weight control in wrestling, selection of first aid equipment, recommending special equipment for those athletes with special handicaps, etc., in addition to those regular duties of team physician.
   Insurance coverage must be available as well as a complete medical history on each athlete. Providing an athletic trainer at practice sessions and games is highly recommended.

FOURTEEN

Developing a Dynamic Cheerleading Program

The purpose of this chapter is to illustrate some of the many facets of a comprehensive cheerleading program. Such areas as clinics and camps, a selection plan, awards system and eligibility, developing a handbook, and promoting school spirit will be discussed.

The real value and importance of sound cheerleading groups cannot be minimized. Like any other phase of the athletic department, this program must be well organized, properly administered, and efficiently operated for lasting results.

CLINICS FOR CHEERLEADERS

State Sponsored Clinics

Most of the states have cheerleading clinics which are sponsored by the state athletic associations. In Ohio, for example, there are five such programs conducted each fall. Four are held at colleges and universities in different parts of the state. One is held in the northeastern district at Berea High School.

These clinics are well advertised and well attended. The programs are held on Saturdays and last all day. Although the management of these clinics is done locally, a nationally known instructor is responsible for the program.

A small fee is charged each girl who participates, which also includes a luncheon. These programs are geared for varsity, junior varsity, and junior high school teams.

The programs include such things as cheerleading techniques, demonstrations of yells by teams in attendance, mass teaching of outstanding routines, clinic summary, etc.

Style shows modeling various types of cheerleading uniforms is always popular. Many good ideas are derived from these displays. Excellent brochures, pamphlets, and books may also be purchased at these programs.

State sponsored clinics are especially beneficial to those teams unable to attend summer camps.

SUMMER CHEERLEADER CAMPS

Attendance at summer cheerleading camps continues to increase each year. The benefits derived and the improved moral of the team are especially worthwhile.

Since most schools do not or cannot help pay for expenses to these camps, cheerleaders often embark on money raising projects for this purpose. Probably the best time to attend summer camps is shortly after school closes in June. This interferes less with vacation, jobs, and summer school classes.

Cheerleaders get many new ideas which they are most anxious to incorporate in their program. Some of the more important aspects being stressed are:

1. Learning "good taste" cheers
2. Learning which cheers to use and not to use
3. Ideas for crowd control
4. Plans for pep rallies
5. Proper uses of megaphones and pom-poms
6. New tumbling and stunt techniques
7. Group lectures with question and answer session

LOCAL CLINICS IN SPRING

Each year in early April, the secondary schools should conduct clinics for all girls interested in trying out for the cheerleading teams. There should be from four to six sessions.

All girls participating in these clinics should have parent permission cards on file before actually taking part in the program.

Varsity and junior varsity squads may work together in clinics but should have separate tryouts for their respective groups.

Graduating senior cheerleaders can give much valuable assistance in instructing these less experienced girls. Senior high advisors must be certain to work closely with the junior high advisors on all of the pertinent details.

CHEERLEADER SELECTION PLAN

Before we can proceed with the selection of cheerleaders we must establish some criteria for the determining of the judges. Each school system may vary in their philosophy in choosing these judges. A number of factors must be considered and should be spelled out in the cheerleading handbook.

The following list may be helpful in obtaining qualified judges, who should be selected at the discretion of the cheerleader advisor.

1) Cheerleader advisor of that team
2) Other physical education teachers or college students majoring in physical education
3) Qualified teachers
4) Athletic Coaches
5) Guidance counselors
6) Former cheerleading coaches

Probably no two schools will follow the same system of selecting judges. Problems can arise from different groups mentioned here or others being used.

Judges should be selected who are capable, interested in the program, and fair in their ratings.

There is no second or third team in cheerleading such as in other sports. Once the final cut is made, we must live by these decisions.

QUALITIES JUDGES LOOK FOR IN TRYOUTS

The general appearance of the cheerleaders is very important and is the first category to be considered. These qualities are especially significant.

1) Be neat, clean, and well groomed.
2) Have a neat and attractive hair style–one that doesn't need constant care with the hands.
3) Good posture.
4) Pleasant smile. Should not be artificial in nature.
5) Never chew gum.
6) Eye contact with the audience.
7) Be self confident and not self-conscious.
8) Poise.

The second area which the judges will consider is that of personality traits. These seven qualities are always relevant.

1) Leadership–ability to lead and control a group, possess dependable judgement, have imagination, initiative and originality.
2) Character–unquestionable reputation, highly respected, high standards of sportsmanship, and a quality representative of school.
3) Loyalty–to the school, to the teams, to the other cheerleaders, and to the coach.
4) Attitude–friendly, courteous, responsible.
5) Cooperation–works well in a group; gets along well with others at school and in the community.
6) Willingness–work hard and steadily throughout the year.
7) Citizenship–a "must" trait for all cheerleaders.

The third phase in the selection of cheerleaders is that of ability. This is sub-divided into two separate categories, namely cheerleading ability and acrobatic ability.

The cheerleading ability will include the following.

1) Pep, enthusiasm, and spirit
2) Coordination–a sense of rhythm and timing with the words
3) Definite arm movements
4) Voice is clearly understood
5) Yelling the cheer is also clearly understood
6) Avoids watching her own motions

The acrobatic ability includes:

1) Cartwheels (straight legs)
2) Splits
3) Specialty

4) Jumps (height and graceful landing)
5) Roundoffs

In the final tryouts it is recommended to have two different sessions. The first session would be devoted to skills only. The chart shown in Figure 14-1 is used for recording these performances.

Each judge will use a separate sheet for each contestant. No cheerleader is introduced by name, but only by number. Everything possible should be done to make the selections as fair and as objective as possible.

The second session in the final tryouts is devoted to cheers. The chart shown in Figure 14-2 is used in judging these performances.

Here also each judge will use a separate sheet for each contestant. Once again the cheerleader is introduced by a number only.

When the final results are tabulated the students who have tried out for the team should be the first to know the results. This is only common courtesy. Some schools give a special flower or insignia to the cheerleaders for them to wear on the day the results are announced on the public address system at school. This or some other similar custom could be followed to honor the cheerleaders for the following year.

Many capable students fail to make the team, and as a result disappointments and sometimes "hard feelings" may follow. In order to help satisfy all who have tried out for the team, the cheerleader coach should make available the results sheets to these students. This helps considerably to eliminate questionable decisions and other suspicion.

AWARD SYSTEM AND ELIGIBILITY

Award System

The policy for cheerleading awards varies considerably with different school districts and in different parts of the country. However since the cheerleaders should be part of the athletic association, the awards system should be somewhat similar to that of other sports.

It is advisable to have uniform awards policies at the junior high school level and again at the senior high school level within the same school district.

In junior high schools the first year award should be a school

CHEERLEADING TRYOUTS
Skills Rating Sheet

Number of Cheerleader________

	1	2	3	4	Comments
JUMPS	X	X	X	X	
baby doll					
SPREAD					
shag					
REQUIRED SKILLS	X	X	X	X	
cartwheel–right					
cartwheel–left					
SPLITS					
roundoff					
slam					
combination					
OPTIONALS	X	X	X	X	
PERSONAL QUALITIES	X	X	X	X	
appearance					
POISE					
posture					

Total ____________

Figure 14-1

CHEERLEADING TRYOUTS
Cheers Rating Sheet

No. of Cheerleader ______

	1	2	3	4
HELLO	X	X	X	X
timing				
motions				
co-ordination				
jump				
HEY SHOW EM	X	X	X	X
motions				
voice				
timing & co-ordination				
jump				
ORIGINAL CHEER				
motions				
words				
timing & co-ordination				
voice				
GROUP CHEER–GO BRAVES				
PERSONAL QUALITIES	X	X	X	X
pep & spirit				
crowd appeal				
appearance				

TOTAL ______________

Figure 14-2

letter with a megaphone insert. The second year award should be a megaphone chain. Certificates may be given in addition to the regular awards.

In the senior high schools the awards policy should include a school letter for the first award. The second year award should be a service bar. If a third year award is given it may be a captain's letter and service bar or a megaphone charm for a girl who was not the captain. Certificates may also be given in addition to the regular award.

Schools having junior varsity cheerleaders may give smaller junior varsity letters or appropriate certificates. If the junior varsity athletes receive numerals, these are recommended for the cheerleaders as well.

Special Groups

Most schools have their regular cheerleaders for the football and basketball seasons. With the ever increasing number of sports, more new cheerleading groups are emerging. Wrestling cheerleaders are a good example of this. Since this season coincides with basketball, the group cannot cheer at both sports.

The addition of special cheerleading groups necessitates more uniforms, more tryouts, and sometimes more coaches. The fact that more girls are involved in a wholesome activity makes it all worthwhile.

The awards system for special groups should be somewhat similar to the regular cheerleaders, even though they only are involved with one sport.

Awards at the junior and senior high schools should be presented at an awards assembly immediately following that particular season.

Eligibility

One of the most controversial aspects of the cheerleading program deals with the policies regarding eligibility. Some athletic directors and principals argue that requirements for cheerleaders should be the same as for all of the other sports. If they are part of the same program, then why have different standards?

Many cheerleader advisors do not agree. They feel that since the competition is so keen, grades can be a factor in selection of these girls. They also believe that the time required to be a cheerleader necessitates an emphasis on good grades. Students who are marginal cases academically cannot be depended upon on frequent occasions. The majority of these problems stems from poor time planning rather than a lack of ability to do good work.

The following policy is in effect in the Berea City Schools concerning eligibility requirements for cheerleaders. This includes the junior and senior high school program.

1) Each girl must have a 2.0 average ("C") based on the first four grading periods. Tryouts are held during the fifth grading period.
2) For each six weeks period, grades will be turned in to the advisor.
3) For each grade of "D" in any subject, the cheerleader will miss as much time as is necessary to bring the grade to a "C".
4) The advisor will make a weekly check of grades for any girl doing questionable work.
5) Any girl receiving a "U" (unsatisfactory) grade in citizenship will be dismissed from the squad until the advisor receives a written statement from the teacher involved, to the effect that she is now satisfactory in this regard.
6) Failure of any course constitutes dismissal from the squad for at least six weeks.
7) In fall tryouts for special groups such as wrestling cheerleaders there must be a 2.0 ("C") average for the first six week period. All other requirements mentioned already will pertain to these groups.

DEVELOPING A HANDBOOK

The development of a cheerleading handbook is most important. Items such as judging, awards, eligibility, etc. already discussed in this chapter would be included. This section will deal with other significant areas.

Summer Practices

Practices held during the summer months are important for several reasons. First, they help mold the squad into a smoother functioning team. Second, they are great morale builders. Third, they enable the cheerleaders to work on many new cheers. Fourth, it is an excellent time to concentrate on skills and to put into use some of the new things learned at camps held in June. Fifth, it helps set the pace for practices held later on in school.

Since the cheerleader advisor is usually not paid for summer practices, she is not held responsible for them. Most cheerleaders are anxious to practice on a required basis of one evening per week. Vacations, jobs, and other activities may interfere with practice. In these cases cheerleaders may be excused. Those who are absent for other reasons will be replaced by the alternate cheerleader.

The captain will be responsible for these practice sessions and shall report to the coach the progress of the squad.

Supervision at Games

The cheerleader advisor is responsible for being at all games, both home and away. If she cannot attend for any reason, she should notify the director of athletics or principal.

Another teacher or coach may take her place. The cheerleader captain should also be informed of this change, as well as parents who may be driving the squad to an away game.

Uniforms

Since the cheerleaders are representatives of the school, they should be dressed accordingly. Too often they appear to be rather scantily clad at football games even in inclement weather. And too often they appear to be overly dressed at indoor events such as basketball and wrestling.

The advisor should be responsible for the purchase of uniforms and other equipment. These items are included in the regular athletic budget, the same as other sports.

Practice Sessions

All regular practice sessions should be well organized and properly planned. Compulsory attendance by all cheerleaders is most important.

Pre-season practices should be conducted two or three times a week. During the season, they may be limited to one per week. When a pep assembly is to be held, one day will be devoted to practice for it.

The advisor should remain at the school following practice until all of the cheerleaders are dressed and out of the building.

Alternates

The role of the alternate is a most difficult one. She is a member of the team, but does not cheer at all of the games. She is required to attend all practice sessions and must meet all of the requirements of the regular cheerleaders.

The alternate takes over under such circumstances as a cheerleader's absence, a grade or other eligibility problem, an injury or illness, etc. She may cheer on other occasions at the coach's discretion.

Her responsibilities include assistance at dances and with pep assemblies, preparing favors for banquets, making posters and signs, and helping with other cheerleading projects.

Junior Varsity Squads

Junior varsity squads are composed of sophomores and juniors in most three year high schools. In four year high schools these teams consist mostly of freshmen and sophomores. Seniors should be used on varsity squads only.

These cheerleaders should be chosen separately from the varsity squads. Tryouts should be held separately and on different evenings.

This squad would cheer at all junior varsity football and basketball games, both home and away. They will also assist the varsity squad at all of the cheerleading activities.

Transportation to Away Games

At the junior high school level, it is highly recommended that the cheerleaders ride the regular team bus. This creates no real problem since most of the trips are fairly close. They should be accompanied by their advisor and sit together in the bus.

At the senior high school level, the situation is different. Many times the trips are long and tiresome. It necessitates an early departure and a late return. In many cases it is not at all practical to take the cheerleaders on the team bus.

The following suggestions may prove helpful.

1) Cheerleaders should ride the student spectator buses when they are offered. This not only provides transportation but helps supply spirit and enthusiasm to and from the games.
2) No students should be permitted to drive the cheerleaders to away games.
3) Mini-buses or station wagons owned by the board of education are ideal for this purpose.
4) Certain designated parents may drive the cheerleaders to these games if no other transportation is available.

PROMOTING SCHOOL SPIRIT

The cheerleader squad can help promote school spirit in a number of ways. In this section of the chapter we will discuss some of the more important concepts.

Pep Assemblies

In most schools the cheerleader advisor and team are responsible for all of the arrangements for pep assemblies. There are certain guidelines which should be followed for best results.

1) The principal should approve the number of pep assemblies before the season begins.
2) The coach in that particular season should be advised of these dates and should be present with his team.
3) Skits should be planned and written by the cheerleaders, then approved by the advisor.
4) Entire program should be typed and given to the teacher in charge of assemblies.
5) Should be held as the last period of the day.

Signs

One of the best means of showing school spirit is reflected through signs and posters. These may be prepared by cheerleaders, pep club members, student council members, and other groups. The signs and posters should be approved by the student council officers or advisor.

A good rule to follow is to have fewer neat displays than a multitude of "sloppy" ones.

Victory Breakfasts

Cheerleader squads working in cooperation with the student council can promote victory breakfasts on Friday mornings before school starts. These consist of donuts, milk, and juice with some brief, well planned cheers thrown in for the main course.

These breakfasts should be inexpensive, supervised, well planned, and publicized. They can then be most successful.

Pep Clubs

Many schools sponsor pep clubs, senior men's clubs, and similar cheering groups. The major objective of these organizations should be the encouragement of the teams, the promotion of school spirit, and the display of good sportsmanship.

If these clubs are to function at their best, they must practice frequently, dress appropriately, and cooperate with the cheerleader squad.

Oftentimes unruly, poorly supervised groups of this kind are a detriment rather than an asset.

Pep clubs should also encourage the other students to cheer and not be exclusive in this regard.

The Mascot

A school mascot can serve a very useful purpose in promoting school spirit. Besides performing at the games, she may assist the cheerleading squad and advisor in some specific projects.

Some of these duties may include letters to visiting cheerleading squads looking forward to meeting them at the game, arrangements for cokes between halves of the game, and pre-game arrangements.

Other Techniques

There are many other ways to promote school spirit. The following ideas have proven to be very successful.

1) Public address announcements before school, between classes, and during the lunch hour.
2) Wearing game jerseys or jackets by team members to

classes on the day of the game. Wearing of cheerleader uniforms on the day of the game.

3) Sending a "good luck" telegram to the team. Each student contributes ten cents to help defray the cost and gets to sign his name.
4) Selling of bumper stickers and decals.
5) Preparation of little bags of candy and fruit for the team as they board the bus for an away game. These may have a slogan written on the bag such as "Beat Maple Heights!"
6) Police escorts to special games.
7) Use of the band and majorettes before, during, and after the games.
8) Well organized and supervised car caravans.
9) Painting of cars.
10) Cannons at football games for use when team has scored.

FIFTEEN

Organizing and Maintaining a Strong Junior High School Athletic Program

One of the most controversial phases of any athletic program deals with the junior high school. School systems vary greatly in their philosophy and in their general attitude in regard to competition for students at this age level.

Many coaches and athletic directors feel that a highly organized program must be put in operation in the upper elementary grades (5th and 6th). Still others believe that this is too early and that ninth grade competition is soon enough.

Different factors help to determine the kind of program that is actually offered. Community interests, facilities available, prior success in certain sports, senior high school league competition, etc. play a major part in this decision. Consultation with the medical profession in this regard is also most important.

This chapter will reflect information from various sources relevant to this topic.

STANDARDS FOR JUNIOR HIGH SCHOOL ATHLETICS

The Junior High School Athletics Sub-Committee of the Joint Committee on Standards for Interscholastic Athletics, sponsored by the American Association for Health, Physical Education, and Recreation, the National Association of Secondary School Principals; and the National Federation of State High School Athletic Associations prepared a report on standards for Junior High School Athletics in 1963. This report is still most helpful in debating the pros and cons of this program. Excerpts of this report follow:

POINTS OF AGREEMENT

Although the opponents and the proponents of interscholastic athletics for boys in junior high schools may vigorously debate several points, they are in general agreement on four basic points.

FIRST, both the opponents and the proponents of junior high school athletics—together with most persons who are interested in the welfare of youth—agree that the sedentary habits of living associated with our mechanized society may seriously impair the fitness of American youth; and that the schools should contribute to the opportunities provided for participation in vigorous physical activities.

SECOND, both the opponents and the proponents agree that all youngsters can profit—educationally, as well as physically—from participation in competitive athletic activities appropriate to their age group.

THIRD, both the opponents and the proponents agree that to provide opportunities for *all* youngsters to profit from participation in athletic activities, the school must provide adequate programs of required physical education, intramurals, and physical recreation.

FOURTH, both the opponents and the proponents agree that athletic competition for youth should be carefully supervised and controlled, and that every effort should be extended to ensure that such competition provides a safe educational experience for the participants.

PROGRAM OF INTERSCHOLASTIC ATHLETICS

1. *The interscholastic athletics program for boys in the junior high school should make definite contributions toward the accomplishment of the educational objectives of the school.*

Primary emphasis should be placed on providing educational experiences for the participants rather than on producing winning teams or providing entertainment for the student body and the patrons of the school. The practice sessions and the athletic contests should be so scheduled that the academic program of the school is not directly or indirectly disrupted. To conserve the time available to the participants for homework, the practice sessions for interscholastic athletics should be relatively short. Under no circumstances should any practice session be longer than ninety minutes. Athletic contests should be held in the afternoons immediately after school hours, rather than at night; and except on rare occasions should be held on the last day of the school week.

The interscholastic athletics program should be so conducted that desirable school citizenship and good sportsmanship are fostered among both participants and spectators.

2. *The interscholastic athletics program for boys in the junior high school should supplement—rather than serve as a substitute for—an adequate program of required physical education, intramurals, and physical recreation for all students.*

If in a school a shortage of facilities, equipment, or personnel with professional training in physical education restricts the quality or the extent of the required physical education program, the intramural program, the physical recreation program, or the interscholastic athletics program that can be offered, the physical education program, the intramural program, and the physical recreation program should hold precedence over the interscholastic program. Under no circumstances should the interscholastic athletics program be provided a disproportionate allotment of time, facilities, or personnel services at the expense of the programs for all boys and girls.

The members of the interscholastic teams should be excused from the required physical education classes only for the class periods in which the activity being presented in the class is the sport in which the members of the interscholastic teams are participating.

3. *The interscholastic athletics program for boys in the junior high school should, under the administration and the supervision of the appropriate school officials, be conducted by men with adequate professional preparation in physical education.*

The interscholastic teams should be coached by certified

teachers—preferably teachers of physical education—who are members of the regular staff of the school in which the coaching is done. For these teachers, the coaching assignments should be considered as part of their regular teaching duties and should be taken into account in the assessing of their total teaching loads.

The administrative policies for the school should require that the teachers who coach interscholastic teams give basic priority to their teaching duties.

The teachers who coach interscholastic teams should possess, in addition to a knowledge of the sports for which they are responsible, a knowledge of (a) child growth and development, (b) the effects of exercise on the human organism, (c) first aid, and (d) the place and purpose of interscholastic athletics in the educational program. They should have at least a minor in physical education.

4. The interscholastic athletics program for boys in the junior high school should be so conducted that the physical welfare of the participants is protected and fostered.

Boxing, as a competitive sport, should be prohibited.

Tackle football—because of its contact aspects, the intensity with which it is played when emotions run rampant, and its relatively high injury rate—presents certain special problems. These problems are intensified in communities where there are pressures to use junior high school athletics as a farm system for the intensive development of high school prospects. Unless these factors can be controlled—and the kind of equipment, facilities, health supervision, coaching, and officiating that are necessary for the optimum safety of the participants can be provided—tackle football should not be included in the junior high school athletics program.

Before being allowed to report for practice or to participate in any phase of interscholastic athletics, each boy should have a thorough medical examination which includes a careful review of his health history. Subsequent medical examinations should be given as needed.

Participants should be furnished with complete, well-fitted protective equipment of the highest quality—not hand-me-downs or equipment of inferior grade.

Individual participants should be allowed to take part in interscholastic contests only after three weeks of physical conditioning and training.

The rules, the equipment, and the playing area for each interscholastic activity should be modified in accordance with the interests and the capacities of junior high school boys, as should the length of the playing season and the number of games played during each season. Under no circumstances should the number of contests played by junior high school teams be greater than half the number played by the senior high school teams. No boy should participate in more than one interscholastic contest a week. Interscholastic tournaments should be prohibited.

A physician should be present during all interscholastic contests in which injuries are likely to occur. Definite procedures for obtaining, without undue delay, the services of a physician to care for injuries that occur during practice sessions should be established.

Participants who have been ill or injured should be readmitted to practice sessions or contests only upon the advice of a physician.

Certified officials should be engaged to officiate at all interscholastic contests.

The welfare of the individual boy should be the basic criterion upon which is determined whether or not the boy should participate in interscholastic athletics.

The controls outlined in the above recommendations are essential to a desirable program of interscholastic athletics in the junior high school. Careful observance of these controls assures optimum protection of the health and safety of the participants. A program of interscholastic athletics for junior high school boys should not be contemplated or continued when conditions or pressures prevent strict adherence to the recommended controls.

MEMBERSHIP IN STATE ATHLETIC ASSOCIATION

There is never much question as to a senior high school's affiliation with the state high school athletic association. The junior high school status has not always been so clear.

In Ohio for example, some schools felt that by not joining the state athletic association they could conduct any program that they so desired on the junior high school level. Since they were not member schools, they could not be penalized. In order to maintain more uniform programs throughout the state, a ruling was made to declare ineligible for his first year of high school competition any boy who had violated a junior high school rule the previous year.

Member schools in Ohio are also covered by a $100,000 catastrophic insurance policy. This includes senior high schools and junior high schools alike. Schools which include grades seven, eight, or nine, or any division of these grades, are eligible to apply for membership in the junior high school division.

A six-year high school operating on a three year plan for high school athletics, grades 10, 11, and 12, may also become a member of the junior high division for grades 7, 8, and 9. A high school operating on a four year plan for high school athletics, grades 9, 10, 11, and 12, may also become a member of the junior high division for grades 7 and 8.

A school shall become a member when its board of education has authorized membership by resolution, and when the principal has signed the prescribed membership blank and the application is approved by the State Board of Control.

The following two sections are taken from the constitution and rules of the Ohio High School Athletic Association. They tend to serve as excellent guidelines in organizing and maintaining a sound junior high school athletic program:

A POINT OF VIEW FOR JUNIOR HIGH SCHOOL ATHLETICS

> The primary function of the junior high school is to provide exploratory experiences which meet the basic criterion for contributing to the goals of general education established for this grade level.
>
> The educational program in the junior high school should be designed particularly to meet the physical, mental, social, and emotional needs of youth during early adolescence. To provide for these needs, the curriculum should offer a core of common experiences which will lead to broad understandings, good citizenship, and acceptable personality adjustment. In addition to the core experiences, many exploratory courses and counseling services should be offered to challenge and stimulate the pupils' desires to acquire more knowledge in specific fields of learning and endeavor. All of the courses offered at the junior high school

level should be flexible enough to allow for individual differences in needs, interests, and abilities.

The goals for the junior high school cannot be fully achieved by the pupil participating only in the required academic program. For this reason each junior high school must provide a broad activity program as part of the curriculum. It is imperative that the junior high school provides each pupil with the opportunity to participate in student activities such as school government, curricular-related club organizations, intramurals, physical fitness programs, and athletic competition.

Educators and health and medical authorities have long recognized that children of the junior high school age have a need for vigorous physical activity to promote normal growth and development. At this age level, there is a real organic need and desire for strenuous physical activity in the form of competitive sports. A study of growth characteristics shows that children of this age seek adventure and vigorous activity, are gregarious and want to belong to a group or team. It is recognized that normal growth and development of children leads them into competitive activities. For these reasons, schools have the responsibility for meeting the developmental needs of boys and girls through programs of physical education which include intramural activities and interschool athletics.

POLICIES AND PRINCIPLES GOVERNING THE ADMINISTRATION OF JUNIOR HIGH SCHOOL ATHLETICS

Competitive interscholastic athletics at the junior high school level has grown enormously in the last few years.

To insure that interscholastic competition will make its maximum contribution to the development of junior high school pupils, it is necessary that the administration of this program be under the jurisdiction of school officials and be carefully supervised by competent and professionally prepared personnel. The organization of interscholastic programs at the junior high school level should be based upon the following principles:

1. The school administrator must accept full responsibility for the proper organization, administration, and supervision of interscholastic athletics as a part of the total educational program.
2. The interscholastic athletic program in the junior high school should supplement, rather than serve as a substitute for, a broad and comprehensive program of physical education and intramural activities for all students.
3. The junior high school interscholastic athletic program should

be considered as a necessary enrichment program for those who excel and will benefit from additional experiences above and beyond the required physical education and intramural programs.

4. The interscholastic program must be developed according to the needs and abilities of the age level of junior high school youth. There should be particular emphasis placed on the health, safety, and personal well-being of the participant, with additional consideration given to the development of wholesome personality and citizenship characteristics.
5. In certain sports it is recommended that serious consideration be given to equalizing competition by some method of classification which will take into consideration individual differences of pupils participating.
6. Whenever feasible, school systems should operate a self-contained junior high interscholastic athletic program rather than schedule distant schools outside of the immediate area.
7. A wide variety of activities should be included in the junior high school interscholastic program and an effort should be made to encourage all pupils to participate.
8. Written policies should be developed at the local level outlining sound administrative practices which will implement state rules and regulations regarding the junior high school interscholastic program.

RULES AND REGULATIONS

The following selected rules and regulations are also taken from the constitution and rules of the Ohio High School Athletic Association. They are very appropriate and can apply to nearly any program in any state.

Grade Limitation–

Elementary pupils not eligible

Pupils below the seventh grade shall not be permitted to compete on any junior high interscholastic athletic team.

Eligibility–

Scholastic Requirements

A pupil to be eligible must have satisfactorily concluded the work in at least 75% of the normal load the preceding semester and be passing in at least 75% of the normal load at the time he participates from the beginning of that semester. A pupil shall be eligible for participation upon certification by the principal.

Administrative Responsibility–

Boys under same administrative head.

All boys on junior high school teams must be enrolled in the same school and be under the supervision of the same principal, and he shall be held ultimately responsible in all matters pertaining to interscholastic athletic activities involving his school.

Semester Attendance Rule–

A boy becomes ineligible for junior high interscholastic athletic competition after he spends two semesters in the ninth grade.

Participation on a High School Team–

A ninth grade boy who has participated as a member of any senior high school team in an interscholastic game in a sport is thereafter ineligible for junior high competition in that sport.

Preliminaries or Exhibitions–

No junior high school interscholastic athletic team or pupils in grades 7, 8, or 9 shall be permitted to participate in preliminary games or exhibitions before, during, or after any college, professional, independent, or interscholastic high school contest in sports recognized by the Ohio High School Athletic Association.

For Operative Purposes–

Four-year high schools that play separate sports schedules for members of the freshman class will follow the regulations for junior high schools in the conduct of athletics at the ninth grade level.

Meets and Tournaments–

TOURNAMENT LIMITATIONS

(a) There shall be no sectional, district, or state meets or tournaments in any junior high school athletic competition. If there is a county meet or tournament, it must be approved by the County Superintendent or the County Athletic Committee. Invitational meets or tournaments must be sponsored by school officials and approved by the Ohio High School Athletic Association.

(b) No Invitational Track Meets or Basketball Tournaments for junior high schools will be approved unless the sponsoring school is a member of OHSAA.

Night Contests–

Contests on Nights Preceding a Day of School

No interscholastic game, meet, or tournament shall be played on a night preceding a school day. A night contest is one starting after 6:00 P.M.

Participating Limitations–

Number of Contests Per Day

(a) A boy shall not participate in more than one interscholastic contest on any one day.

(b) Rule16, Section 3a and b on page 36, is applicable in this section. Therefore, if a boy plays two quarters in an eighth grade game and two quarters in a ninth grade game on the same day, he has participated in one interscholastic contest.

Officials–

REGISTERED OFFICIALS

One or more registered officials should be used in all interscholastic contests.

Safety Measures–

SAFETY REGULATIONS

In order to assure junior high school contestants the optimum of protection against injury to their bodies and to their health, the following minimum regulations shall be enforced:

A. Physical Examination–Athletic participation forms properly signed by a physician, by the participant, and by one of his parents or guardians must be on file with the administrator before any candidate for a team may participate in a practice. These forms necessitate the physician's certification of the individual's physical fitness no less than once each school year.

B. Conditioning Period–To insure good physical condition of participants, each boy shall have at least fifteen days of practice and conditioning before engaging in any interscholastic contest.

C. Equipment–Proper equipment and safety precautions must be stressed, such as properly fitted protective clothing, pads, shoes, helmets with face guards, etc. Whenever possible, properly fitted tooth and mouth protectors should be provided.

D. Facilities–The physical facilities such as playing areas, locker and shower rooms, bleachers, etc., shall be designed and maintained to safeguard the health and safety of all participants and spectators.

JUNIOR HIGH SCHOOL PROGRAM OFFERED

The type of junior high school program that is offered should certainly be one of balance and one in which a large number of students may participate.

A well balanced program could include two sports in the fall, two in the winter, and two in the spring. Fall sports are football and cross-country. Winter sports are basketball and wrestling. Spring sports are baseball and track.

Squads should be large and well equipped. The type of coaches selected for this age level must never be minimized. The head coaches in the junior high schools should be second in ability, experience, and knowledge only to the head coaches in the senior high schools.

A real effort must be made in staffing so that sufficient importance is placed in the work to be done at each level. Many coaches are not interested in any positions except in the high school program. This is due largely to stipends paid, glamour attached to the high school program, etc. Some teachers feel the same way and want to move up to the supposedly more sophisticated senior high school departments. Much of this prestige barrier may be removed by a close, well-knit association between the two levels.

In order to insure large squads we must be certain of several procedures.

First, sell your coaches on the value of large squads.

Second, do not cut boys from the teams unless absolutely necessary. In football there may not be enough equipment for every boy. In basketball the numbers may be too great to retain all of the boys aspiring to make the squad.

Third, encourage boys who are cut from the squad to compete in the intramural program. They should be encouraged to try again the following year.

Fourth, attempt to have a staff large enough to work with large groups.

Fifth, get as many boys in actual game competition as possible. The Berea City Schools and the Parma City Schools are scheduling football games for boys who do not actually play in a regularly scheduled game. There are officials, spectators, cheerleaders, etc. just as for the regular games. In sports like track, run extra heats for boys not competing in the regular races. In wrestling match up boys not participating in the normal weight classes, giving them opportunities for game-like competition. This taste of competition, of "getting in the game," is a great morale builder and one of the best sellers of our program.

Earlier in this chapter mention was made of not starting the program too early and of not waiting too long. In the opinion of many athletic directors the program should begin with complete competition in the eighth and ninth grades. The seventh grade can be one of encouraging these students to participate in a large intramural program encompassing a number of activities.

It is also highly recommended to keep the eighth and ninth grade teams separate if at all possible. Basically the ninth grade teams should be for ninth graders and the eight grade teams for eighth graders. Even if an eighth grade boy has more ability than a ninth grader, he should not be moved up, and in turn bump an older boy off that team. Such moves can kill off the enthusiasm for the ninth graders and can add to the "cocksureness" of the eighth graders.

A similar problem may be encountered if seventh and eighth graders are lumped together on one team. Sometimes because of the size of the school it is necessary to group these teams together. Even so, coaches must work toward the success of the overall program, rather than immediate results.

ASSOCIATION WITH OTHER SCHOOLS

There is no better place to begin stressing the significance of good sportsmanship than in the junior high school program. Coaches, players, and students alike must constantly work to keep their attitude and behavior above reproach.

The type of hospitality that we extend to the visiting schools is always important. This will range from clean dressing rooms that are available when the visiting teams arrive, to common courtesy and respect at all times.

Provisions should be made for medical attention in the event of an injury. Many times we are lax about these matters in the junior high school program.

Oftentimes there is little conformity in rules, events, weight classes, etc. Scheduling should be done with schools where specific rules and regulations are applied.

State high school athletic associations can help greatly in this regard. Most junior high schools want, and need, more than suggestions or guidelines. Athletic directors should work closely with state commissioners to be certain that junior high schools have proper rules to play by in all sports.

Some of the state high school athletic associations are adding assistant commissioners to their staffs with specific assignments in junior high school work. This is a giant step in the right direction and should help materially in upgrading the program.

In games and events of a special nature it is highly recommended that definite instructions to both schools be clearly spelled out. The following information sheet is a typical example:

To: Principals, Faculty Managers, Football Coaches of Roehm and Ford Junior High Schools

From: Bob Purdy, Director of Athletics

Subject: Roehm–Ford Stadium Game–Date–Ray E. Watts Stadium

The following items should cover most of the details concerning this game:

1. Ford is the host school, will use the home stands and benches, pay the officials and furnish the game ball.
2. Mr. Purdy will arrange for two policemen–one for each side of the field.
3. A doctor will be in attendance and will sit on the home team bench.
4. Mr. Purdy is having 2,000 25¢ student pre-sale tickets printed for sale. Each school will keep its own student pre-sale. All tickets at the gate are 50¢.

5. Mr. Purdy will arrange for the operation of the concessions stand, with the profits to be split equally.
6. Phones will be set up for both teams as in the past.
7. Ford will furnish the necessary gate help for Maple St. and Bagley Road gates. We should be open for ticket sales by 1:00.
8. Mr. Purdy will arrange for a scoreboard operator and a public address announcer.
9. Dressing rooms are available for both teams.
10. Each school should help with crowd control.
11. No Berea or Midpark High football player will be admitted free unless he is on a list at the gate.
12. Net gate receipts will be shared equally. Checks for officials will be the only game expense to the competing schools.

One of the best procedures to follow is to conduct meetings of the coaching staffs with the director of athletics prior to the start of each season. If major changes in policies are being considered, the junior high school principals should also be included in these meetings. The agenda may include problem areas that need attention, implementation of new ideas, eligibility procedures, possible equipment changes, etc.

At the junior high school level, competition in leagues or conferences should be discouraged. This is not to imply that a group of area schools should not work together in scheduling games in all sports. Playing for a championship at this age is just not good. Play to win, to go undefeated–yes. But leave the championships for the high school teams.

Most schools find that concluding a season with a relay meet or a tournament is very beneficial. This could include such events as a four or eight team basketball tournament, a four or eight team wrestling tournament, an invitational or relay track and field meet, or a small baseball tournament. Activities such as these should be well organized, properly structured, and efficiently managed. Junior high school events are important and should be conducted accordingly.

SIXTEEN

Professional Growth and Participation in State and National Associations

The importance of position of the secondary school athletic director continues to grow in most school systems. It is rapidly becoming one of the key administrative jobs for several reasons.

First, the principal, who is responsible for all departments in his particular building, no longer has the time to supervise and administer the athletic program.

Second, the expansion of the present program to include girls' interscholastic athletics, intramural activities, and related clubs and organizations.

Third, the coordination of the junior high school programs with the senior high programs needs much attention.

Fourth, the importance of overseeing the many phases of the program as to supervision of coaches, policies and procedures, facilities, finance, transportation, insurance, police protection, and medical care is most significant.

Fifth, very few other positions in education have more association with agencies and groups outside the school system.

His dealings include game officials, other schools and their personnel, boosters clubs, the state athletic association, physicians, police departments, etc.

PROFESSIONAL PREPARATION OF ATHLETIC DIRECTORS

The unfortunate fact is that many directors of athletics are given these positions with little or no experience or training which will assist them with their job. Most of them are teaching several classes a day. Many schools have no written policies and procedures to serve as guidelines. The results are quite obvious.

Since athletic programs are continually growing and since the director's role becomes more important, the significance of proper preparation is only logical. Ohio University in Athens, Ohio, has been a pioneer in this field. They offer an excellent graduate study program in sports administration. The curriculum covers training in interscholastic and intercollegiate athletic administration and facility management as well. The expanded program includes courses related specifically to the student's area of interest. He will get much needed specialized training in the broad overview of business as a whole.

In addition to advanced graduate courses, the student must spend an academic quarter on an internship with either a big city school district, a college or university, or a professional sports organization.

Some of the early graduates of this program have fine positions in public relations in promotional work as ticket directors, etc. with professional football and baseball teams. It goes without saying that many of these graduates will enter the field of education well trained in areas that most athletic directors in today's schools sorely lack.

The impetus to develop graduate programs for the professional preparation of athletic directors should come from state athletic directors associations, from the American Association of Health, Physical Education, and Recreation, and from the National Federation of Secondary School Athletic Associations. These groups should approach institutions of higher learning to encourage the development of such programs.

The Professional Preparation Panel of thee AAHPER has endorsed a document entitled "Professional Preparation of the Administrator of Athletics," a comprehensive recommendation by a committee which studied this problem for several years. The statement was published in the September 1970 issue of the JOURNAL OF HEALTTH, PHYSICAL EDUCATION, RECREATION.

A committee of the American Association of Health, Physical Education and Recreation prepared a report in 1968 on professional preparation of the administrator of athletics. This included a section on competencies and content at the graduate level, which is listed in Figure 16-1.

Professional preparation programs should be specialized yet flexible enough to meet the needs of each student. Time should not be spent in training health and physical education supervisors or specialists in this area. Some of these courses are valuable, but the education of a director of athletics in his particular role is vital.

CERTIFICATION OF SECONDARY SCHOOL COACHES

The proper certification and professional preparation of secondary school coaches not wishing to enter the field of physical education is no new concern. This problem, in fact, has existed for nearly forty years and actually has no easy solution. As has already been referred to in an earlier chapter, it is extremely difficult to fill all coaching positions by getting the man we want, who can coach what we want, who can teach what we need, in the building where we want him. Most school administrators want coaches teaching in their major fields. This is understandable, but creates a further problem.

The certification of these coaches, as important as it is, can further compound the problem.

The Division of Men's Athletics of the American Association for Health, Physical Education, and Recreation, and the National Council of State High School Coaches Associations published an excellent booklet in 1971 on Certification of High School Coaches.

Dr. Matthew G. Maetozo, Director of the Division of Health, Education and Physical Education at Lock Haven State College in Lock Haven, Pennsylvania, gives an excellent insight to this problem in discussing standards of professional preparation for athletic coaches in this publication. We quote the following:

Individuals and professional associations might differ due to

Competencies	Content (To include such things as)
1. An awareness and understanding of the role of athletics in education and our society and the rules, regulations, policies and procedures of the various governing bodies	1. a. Historical aspects b. Cultural aspects c. Philosophical aspects d. Ethics e. Interrelationships with physical education f. Interrelationships with women's sports programs g. Professional and related organizations
2. An awareness and understanding of sound business procedures as related to athletic administration	2. a. Accounting practices b. Budget and finance c. Purchasing policies d. Operational policies e. Fund raising
3. An awareness and understanding of administrative problems as related to equipment and supplies	3. a. Purchasing b. Design c. Renovation d. Maintenance e. Inventory
4. An awareness and understanding of problems related to facilities (indoor and outdoor)	4. a. Planning b. Construction c. Maintenance d. Multiple use
5. An awareness and understanding of school law and liability	5. a. Personal liability b. Institutional liability c. Transportation d. Insurance
6. An awareness and understanding of the factors involved in the conduct of athletic events	6. a. Contracts b. Scheduling c. Travel d. Game management e. Ticket sales f. Promotions g. Tournaments

Figure 16-1

Figure 16-1 *(continued)*

Competencies	Contents (To include such things as)
	h. Spectator control i. Officiating j. Programs
7. An awareness and understanding of good public relations techniques	7. a. Communication media b. Individual and group relationships c. Oral and written communications d. Audio-visual techniques
8. An awareness and understanding of staff relationships	8. a. Professional status b. Staff morale c. Selection d. Promotion e. Salary f. Tenure g. Supervision h. Policies i. Communications j. In-service training
9. An awareness and understanding of the health aspects of athletics	9. a. Medical supervision b. First aid c. Care and prevention of injuries d. Nutrition e. Safety procedures f. Conditioning policies g. Relationship with health services h. Medical insurance
10. An awareness and understanding of the psychological and sociological aspects of sports	10. Effects of competition as they affect the individual, teams, student body and related groups.
11. An awareness and understanding of the need for the interpretation of research	11. a. Studies in athletics b. Studies in sports medicine c. Studies in administration

varying backgrounds and experience, philosophies of education, and involvement at different educational levels in diverse types of schools. All teachers, coaches, and administrators need not come to exactly the same conclusions on a topic of importance. However, there are certain professional practices which should be standardized to ensure optimum advantages for athletes, coaches, school authorities, and involved professional associations. Sufficient consensus should be established in order to provide appropriate direction and progress.

Whether or not coaches of athletics should have completed a major or minor in health and physical education is not of primary concern. The important point is whether the coach possesses the necessary qualifications, background, and preparation to execute the duties of his position. The vast majority of professional groups involved in recent studies believes that professional preparation should include specifically appraised competencies beyond those represented by traditional teacher certification.

Minimum specific professional preparation has not been specified in most states, although there is considerable agreement concerning the areas of preparation, competency, and experience necessary for coaching. Agreement in professional preparation focuses on the following in various combinations: (1) biological sciences (anatomy, physiology, physiology of exercise, and kinesiology); (2) safety, first aid, training and conditioning, and care and prevention of injuries; (3) philosophy, principles, organization, and psychology; (4) theory and techniques of coaching in selected sports.

In various studies, coaches have identified the following areas as requiring greater emphasis: legal responsibilities peculiar to athletics; technical information in the chosen sport to include coaching technique; desirable procedures in squad management and organization; the best methods of developing, training and conditioning athletes; the essentials of bodily movement and effect under stress; and administrative aspects of budget, records, scheduling, and purchase. It is interesting to note that school administrators primarily indicated similar concerns.

Another major area, coaching experiences, should be structured more extensively. At present, planned opportunities for directed experiences are strictly limited. Laboratory experiences in coaching must be further developed during student teaching assignments. Undergraduate and graduate assistantships in sport should be available. Campus and community internships should be considered as one approach to the problem. Involvement in other related experiences would prove highly beneficial; these experiences would include officiating contests, working with co-curricular clubs, or class assignments and seasonal exposure to playground, summer camps, youth organizations, and schools requesting voluntary assistance. Colleges and universities should consider regulations which encourage participation in selected sports for prospective coaches.

It is surprising that a number of high school coaches never participated in the sport being coached while attending secondary school. As college undergraduates, an even greater percentage of coaches never participated in the sport being coached.

Now is the time for professional groups in the various states to strive for certification or endorsement requirements beyond what is now requisite for teaching certification. Plans should be formulated in those states that have not given attention to this area of education; the states that have formulated plans should aggressively pursue implementation. The few states that have requirements in effect should review them in light of the fact that these requirements can vary widely, from having coaches complete a major or minor in physical education to requiring only that coaches satisfactorily complete a course in first aid.

In some states, the colleges and universities are responsible for recommending certification of students who have completed requirements in specific programs. In other states, prerequisites for certification are prescribed by the department of education. In either case or variations thereof, college and university departments, divisions, or schools of health, physical education, and athletics should consider, prepare, and institute approved programs for interschool coaching certification in conjunction with state departments of education.

As states institute requirements for coaches, there should be identification of and agreement upon future dates for enforcement of standards (without retroactive policy). Schools, colleges, universities, and certifying agencies must have reasonable time in which to prepare for implementation.

Since the coach without proper preparation or training can be confronted with problems of health and safety of the athletes, concerns of negligence, and other comparable situations, what plan for certification should he follow?

Dr. Arthur A. Esslinger, Dean of the School of Health, Physical Education, and Recreation, at the University of Oregon, proposes the following plan for certification of high school coaches. This appears in the same American Association for Health, Physical Education, and Recreation publication.

Medical Aspects of Athletic Coaching (3 semester hours)

I. Medical Aspects
II. Protective Equipment and Facilities
III. Training
IV. Injuries
V. Medical and Safety Problems
VI. In-Service Training–Care of the Athlete
VII. Medical Research Related to Athletics

Principles and Problems of Coaching (3 semester hours)

I. Personal Relationships
II. Organization (contest management, athletic equipment, finances, etc.)
III. Important Considerations (Training rules, coaching ethics, etc.)

Theory and Techniques of Coaching (6 semester hours)

I. Educational Implications of the Sport
II. Fundamentals Detailed
III. Technical Information
IV. Scouting
V. Conditioning for a Specific Spot
VI. Organization and Management
VII. Practice Sessions
VIII. Safety Aspects of Particular Sport
IX. Rules and Regulations
X. Evaluation

Kinesiological Foundations of Coaching (2 semester hours)

I. Anatomical Factors
II. Mechanics of Movement

Physiological Foundations of Coaching (2 semester hours)

I. Physiological Factors
II. Exercise Physiology Factors

Several states are already in the process of implementing or establishing requirements for interscholastic coaches. The proper certification and training for these men is a great step forward in professional growth.

DISTRICT, STATE, AND NATIONAL ASSOCIATIONS

National Movement

One of the greatest thrusts in the professional growth of athletic directors took place in January, 1969, in Washington, D. C. It was at that time that over 250 athletic directors were selected to attend a national meeting in the N. E. A. Building. Each of the fifty states were represented.

The purpose of the four day meeting was to exchange ideas of current concern in today's athletic program and to receive insight and assistance in more effectively doing our jobs.

At that time only six states had athletic directors' associations at the state level. Reports were given by these representatives as to the work being done in their states, how they were organized, etc. Many other outstanding speakers discussed such problems as public relations, legal implications, financing athletic programs, etc.

From this meeting, sponsored by the Division of Men's Athletics of the National Association of Health, Physical Education, and Recreation, and other leading professional educational associations, stemmed the formation of the National Council of Secondary School Athletic Directors.

The National Council, in two short years, not only got itself organized but helped form or started to form twenty-one additional state athletic directors associations and conducted six regional conferences throughout the nation. "The Athletic Director," an informative periodic newsletter, is made available to all members and on occasion to all athletic directors in the United States. Publications such as "Crowd Control in High School Athletics" were sponsored by this association.

State Associations

Two of the state athletic directors' associations began in the late

1950's, with New Jersey and Ohio being the pioneers. Indiana, Michigan, Illinois, and Iowa were formed a few years later.

The purpose of these associations is to work together on problems pertinent to that state and to conduct annual professional meetings for the entire membership.

The state associations are similar in organization and yet unique in other aspect, depending on the state. These groups cooperate closely with the individual state athletic associations in rules and regulations pertaining to their states, in serving as representatives on district and state boards of control, and in other matters to help promote better athletics on the state level.

The state athletic directors' associations also cooperate with the National Council of Secondary School Athletic Directors in matters pertaining to professional growth. Largely through the efforts of these groups, regional conferences including as many as seven to twelve states are conducted.

The purposes of regional conferences are:

1. To recommend administrative procedures that will add greater significance to the contributions of the interscholastic athletics program in meeting the purposes of secondary education.
2. To provide a regional forum for the exchange of current practices in secondary school athletic administration.
3. To discover current and evolving trends in athletic administration.
4. To discuss the role of the NCSSAD and the state athletic directors' associations in cooperative projects with other national and state associations.

Such regional meetings help solidify state groups and serve the needs of areas where state associations have not as yet been formed.

District Associations

Most states are not divided into district associations. Ohio followed the state athletic association plan for its structure. It has six districts, with directors from each district serving as members of the state executive board along with the other officers.

District meetings are held as often as twice a year and are well attended. These are in addition to the annual state meetings.

The Northeastern District in Ohio is composed of fourteen counties. They are presently working on plans for annual meetings in each county. Workshops and clinics at the district level can do much for professional growth in these areas. This is especially significant since many of these schools compete against each other on a regular basis.

Policies Governing the Attendance at Clinics and Meetings

One of the most frequently asked questions at meetings of athletic directors revolves around the policy of your particular school system in regard to attendance at clinics, workshops, conventions, etc. The problem becomes quite complex with ever-expanding athletic staffs, more and better professional meetings to attend, and the general financial squeeze facing most schools today.

Before actually adopting policies to cover such meetings, it is always advisable to take a good look at the general philosophy of the school and of the athletic department. Since all sports are important, we should make every effort to allow for all head coaches in the high schools to attend at least one meeting each year. The meetings they attend will be determined in part by the money available and the proximity of that particular occasion.

If at all possible the board of education should pay the necessary expenses and also employ a substitute to take the classes being missed. This is very important since we in athletics believe that our program is in the mainstream of the educational curriculum. This being the case, then the athletic department should be given the same treatment as the other departments.

Some athletic departments have sufficient funds to more than adequately pay clinic expenses, and as a result prefer it this way. If possible, the assistant coaches should be included in some of these meetings.

The junior high coaches are oftentimes left in an awkward position. They are a vital part of the staff and yet may be in different buildings with little or no funds available for clinics or meetings.

By trial and error the coaches soon realize the best meetings to attend and should be given the option of making their own selection within the framework of the overall policy.

What items should be considered and included in policies governing such meetings? The following list may prove helpful:

1. Involve the board of education and superintendent to help determine the policies, and for financial assistance if at all possible.
2. Include at least the head coaches in all sports. Take the assistants and junior high coaches if possible.
3. If board of education funds are not available, clinic expenses should be a definite part of the athletic department budget.
4. Arrange for substitute teachers to cover the classes, unless competent student teachers are available.
5. Report back to staff and administration on the meeting highlights. The sharing of this information can be most beneficial.
6. Conduct your own workshops by using local staff members and other capable people from the area. This can involve many of your own coaches unable to attend meetings elsewhere.
7. Attend state athletic association workshops when possible. These are usually well organized, have good speakers, and operate at a reasonable cost.
8. Periodically reappraise this part of the program and make necessary adjustments.

Professional Behavior of Athletic Directors

In Chapter 1 the professional responsibility of the athletic director was discussed in detail. The professional behavior of the athletic director seems to add the final ingredient of a position which reflects dignity and respect.

Athletics can prosper only when they merit the support and trust of the community. The proper administration of athletic programs influences favorably the general public and the other school officials.

Every member of a profession carries a responsibility to act in a manner becoming a professional person. This implies that each athletic director has an inescapable obligation to abide by the ethical standards of his profession. The behavior of each is the concern of all. The conduct of any athletic director influences the attitude of the public toward athletics in general.

The policies of ethical behavior are designed to inspire a quality of behavior that reflects honor and dignity on the profession. They are not intended as inflexible rules or unchangeable laws. They serve to measure the propriety of an athletic director's behavior in his working relationships. They encourage and emphasize those positive attributes of professional conduct which characterize strong and effective leadership.

The policies to govern the ethical professional behavior of Ohio High School Athletic Directors follow. The preamble and policies which are listed have been a definite asset in maintaining high quality programs throughout the state.

POLICIES

TO GOVERN THE ETHICAL PROFESSIONAL BEHAVIOR OF OHIO SCHOOL ATHLETIC DIRECTORS

PREAMBLE

Athletic programs are an integral part of the total school program and as such must be considered with respect and dignity. Athletics will prosper only if they earn this respect through the character and quality of their administration. Therefore, it behooves all athletic directors to exercise professional leadership.

Our democratic society demands of any group, that claims the status of a profession, to prove itself by being governed through the establishment of ethical policies controlling the actions of its members. This obligation can be achieved through membership and participation in the Ohio High School Athletic Directors Association.

Each member of a profession is responsible to act in a professional manner. This means that the athletic director must abide by the ethical standard of his profession.

These policies are designed to inspire a high quality of ethical behavior and are not meant as inflexible or unchangeable rules. They measure the propriety of an athletic director and encourage and emphasize attributes of professional conduct to develop effective leadership.

THE ATHLETIC DIRECTOR

POLICY I

Must uphold the honor and dignity of his profession in all his relations with students, colleagues, administrators, and the public. He must act impartially in the execution of basic policies; the enforcement of rules and regulations; and to recognize the worth and dignity of all his staff members.

POLICY II

Obeys local, state, and national laws, and holds himself to high ethical and moral standards by constantly displaying a high degree of moral stability and by abiding to the letter of the law in all transactions. He must exert an effort to set an example to foster and respect all rules and regulations pertinent to administration of athletic programs.

POLICY III

Accepts the responsibility to master and to contribute to the growing body of specialized knowledge, concepts, and skills which characterize athletics as a profession.

POLICY IV

Strives to provide the finest possible athletic experiences and opportunities to all students in his school through a comprehensive athletic program.

POLICY V

Carries out in a good faith all policies duly adopted by the school administration and the regulations of his state association, and offers professional service to the best of his ability.

POLICY VI

Recognizes that the athletic programs are an integral part of the total educational program and seeks to keep the school administrators and the public fully and honestly informed about these programs.

SUMMARY:

High Standards of ethical behavior for athletic directors are essential and are compatible with his faith in the power of athletic programs and his commitment to leadership in the preservation and strengthening of the athletic program.

The athletic director must face squarely these beliefs:

1. The effectiveness of the athletic program is his responsibility.
2. Sound athletic programs must have the best trained instructors possible and must be geared to protect the health and safety of the participants.
3. In the final analysis, the athletic director will be judged on the effort he puts forth to improve the quality of the athletic program.

The National Council of State High School Coaches Associations has developed an excellent code of ethics which follows:

NATIONAL CODE OF ETHICS FOR HIGH SCHOOL COACHES

As A Professional Educator

I WILL Exemplify the highest moral character, behavior, and leadership

Respect the integrity and personality of the individual athlete

Abide by the rules of the game in letter and in spirit

Respect the integrity and judgment of sports officials

Demonstrate a mastery of and continuing interest in coaching

Encourage a respect for all athletics and their values

Display modesty in victory and graciousness in defeat

Promote ethical relationships among coaches

Fulfill responsibilities to provide health services and an environment free of safety hazards

Encourage the highest standards of conduct and scholastic achievement among all athletes

Seek to inculcate good health habits including the establishment of sound training rules

Strive to develop in each athlete the qualities of leadership, initiative, and good judgement

The professional growth of athletic directors and coaches has done much to improve the quality and standards of interscholastic athletics throughout the nation.

FUTURE TRENDS IN SCHOOL ATHLETICS

Many new and exciting trends help to make the future athletic programs for secondary schools most promising. Despite the numerous problems of crowd control, financing the programs, adequate facilities, well-trained staff, etc., interscholastic athletics will move ahead.

Exactly what can we expect? The following list can give us some insight as to the future. First, a girls' program comparable in size and scope to that of the boys.

Second, more schedules and more teams at each level of the existing program. For example, varsity reserve teams comprised mainly of juniors not capable enough to play in the varsity games. This team should not be confused with the junior varsity or sophomore team.

Third, more boys retained on each squad at all levels.

Fourth, expansion of present intramural programs to include clubs and organizations needing assistance and direction. Such groups as ski clubs, gymnastics clubs, bowling clubs, etc., could be included.

Fifth, continuation of the program beyond the normal nine month school year to include summer activities of various kinds.

Sixth, scheduling of regular games with officials for players on junior high school teams who do not normally see game action.

Seventh, more and more funding of programs by the local boards of education where lack of revenue has hurt the program.

Eighth, general improvement of facilities and expansion of programs in the inner-city school systems.

Ninth, new programs to include handicapped youngsters at all ages.

Tenth, more and better after school programs for elementary school children. These would be arranged primarily on an intramural basis and should be well supervised.

The more young people become involved in worthwhile athletic programs the less likely they are to be enticed into joining other questionable groups.

Dr. Paul W. Briggs, Superintendent of the Cleveland Public Schools, recently had his research staff conduct a study on dropouts for boys who participated in their athletic program. The following quote easily indicates the great need for larger and better programs, especially in the inner-city. This also appeared as part of an article by Dr. Briggs in the August 1970 issue of *The Coach.*

> Let's look at one school in an area that's really beyond description: In an area where tonight none of us can walk three blocks without in some way being molested; an area of violence and spoiling and trouble on every campus; an area where the police are in trouble and do not get out of their squad cars without being accompanied; an area where the children come to school hungry, poorly kept, and an area that is over-populated and over-crowded. Let's look at what happened in this school; out of 161 boys who had gone out for football, in this school where

over 50% drop out, the record shows that not one had dropped out of school, not one. And twelve of these boys had gone on to college scholarships.

There were 45 in basketball and not a single drop out. Eighteen of these basketballers went on to college scholarships. Now these are kids who should not, by the record, even finish high school.

There were 89 track and not one dropped out of school. Nine of the track boys got college scholarships.

There were 32 in tennis, and one drop out.

In baseball, we had 64 with one drop out, and 3 were drafted by professional teams.

In other words, if we look at the record of that school with 391 athletes, we find two dropouts, and we should have expected more than 40% dropouts. You see why I have to be for athletics? Can I be against athletics tonight, even though I didn't play?

Now, if this had happened just in one school in Cleveland it might be a little different.

Let's look at another school: 140 participants in one sport without a dropout, 100 in basketball with only five dropouts over a five year period. In this second school, 150 participants in football with only eight dropouts.

Another school in our city, 22 full time scholarships in two years, with 400 boys in athletic activities, and of the 400 we didn't lose a single kid. Every one of those 400 athletes stayed to graduate.

FELLOWSHIP OF CHRISTIAN ATHLETES

Just as athletics helps young men to stay in school today and finish their education, so it offers a further challenge to still others. The opportunities for athletes to promote good sportsmanship and good citizenship are not new.

The formation of "Fellowship of Christian Athletes" chapters in our secondary schools and colleges is relatively new. This organization provides opportunities for young men to grow spiritually and to set high moral standards for the entire student body. The primary objective of this group is to bring young athletes into a close fellowship with Christ and their fellowmen (which I have found to be of supreme importance in my own life).

Bibliography

Abinanti, Abby, "The Communications Media and Women in Sports", *Journal Health, Physical Education, Recreation,* Washington, D. C. January 1971.

Alderson, C. J., "Officials and Coaches Are on the Same Team", *Journal of Health, Physical Education and Recreation,* Washington D. C., November, 1963.

Alley, Louis E., "Standards for Junior High School Athletics", *Administration of High School Athletics–Report of a National Conference,* American Association for Health, Physical Education, and Recreation, Washington, D. C., December 1962.

Appenzeller, Herbert, "Play It Safe", *The Athletic Director,* National Council of Secondary School Athletic Directors Association, June, 1971.

Appenzeller, Herbert, *From the Gym to the Jury*, Michie Company, Charlottesville, Virginia, 1970.

Athletic Field and Court Diagrams, Wilson Sporting Goods Co. 24th revised edition, February, 1969.

Athletic Institute, "Youth Baseball Survey for 1965", *Sportscope,* October, 1965.

Barnes, Samuel E., "Sports Clubs", *Journal of Health, Physical Education, Recreation,* Washington, D. C., March, 1971.

"Basic Issues–Should High School Coaches Be Teachers of Physical Education or Teachers of Some Academic Subject?", *Journal of Health, Physical Education, Recreation,* January, 1962.

Baughman, M. D., *Educator's Handbook of Stories, Quotes and Humor,* Parker Publishing Co., West Nyack, N.Y., 1963.

Bell, Mary M., "Are We Exploiting High School Girl Athletics?", *Journal of Health, Physical Education, Recreation,* Washington, D. C., February, 1970.

Benhase, Carl, *Ohio High School Football,* Parker Publishing Co., West Nyack, N. Y., 1971.

Bird, Patrick J., "Tort Liability", *Journal of Health, Physical Education, Recreation,* Washington, D. C., January, 1970.

Blount, Joe M., "Letter-Award Point System", *Scholastic Coach,* January, 1962.

Bontemps, Arnd W., *"Famous Negro Athletes",* Dodd, Mead, and Co. New York, N. Y., 1964.

Boyle, Robert H., "Sport–Mirror of American Life", Little, Brown, and Co. Boston, Mass., 1963.

Brailsford, Dennis, "Sport and Society", University of Toronto Press, Buffalo, N. Y., 1969.

Briggs, Paul W., "We've Got To Take a New Look", *The Coach,* Austin, Texas, August, 1970.

Briggs, Paul W., "The Opportunity To Be Relevant", *Journal Health, Physical Education, Recreation,* Washington, D. C. May, 1970.

Brown, B. J., *Complete Guide to Prevention and Treatment of Athletic Injuries,* Parker Publishing Co., West Nyack, N. Y., 1972.

Bubas, Vic, "Selling Yourself in a New Situation", *Scholastic Coach,* December, 1961.

Cerney, J. V., *Complete Book of Athletic Taping Techniques,* Parker Publishing Co., West Nyack, N. Y., 1972.

Certification of High School Coaches, American Association Health Physical Education, and Recreation Task Force, Washington, D. C., 1971.

Cheerleading Handbook, Berea City Schools, Berea, Ohio, 1971.

Cohn, Robert, and Ball, Steve, Jr., "The High Cost of Winning", *NACDA Quarterly,* Cleveland, Ohio, Winter, 1969.

Cotton, John K., "A Brief For Girls' Athletics", *The Athletic Director* National Council of Secondary Athletic Directors, Washington, D. C., June, 1970.

Crowd Control for High School Athletics, American Association Health, Physical Education, and Recreation, Washington, D. C., August 1970.

Curran, John P., "Primer of Sports Injuries", Charles C. Thomas Publisher, Springifled, Ill., 1968.

Dauer, Victor P., and Schaub, Howard, "Communications Between Physicians and Educators", *Journal Health, Physical Education, Recreation,* Washington, D. C., December, 1970.

DeBacy, Diane L., Spaeth, Ree, Busch, Roxanne, "What Do Men Really Think About Athletic Competition for Women?", *Journal Health, Physical Education, Recreation* Washington, D. C. November, December, 1970.

"Desirable Athletic Competition for Children of Elementary School Age",–A policy Statement–*American Association for Health, Physical Education, and Recreation,* Washington, D. C., 1968.

Dubas, Rene, "Human Ecology", *Journal of Health, Physical Education, Recreation,* Washington, D. C., March, 1970.

Dunn, Ted E., "Coach of Athletics", *The Physical Educator,* December, 1961.

"Encyclopedia of Sport Sciences and Medicine", The American College ot Sports Medicine, The Macmillan Company, New York, New York, 1970.

Fagan, Clifford B., "It's Your Privilege", *The Letterman,* February, 1970.

Fagan, Clifford B., "The Moment of Truth", *The Ohio High School Athlete,* Columbus, Ohio, May, 1970.

Finnigan, Edward, "Eddie Finnigan's Sports Philosophy and Physical Training Tips", Gerald Conway, and Co. Inc., 1968.

Forsythe, Charles E., *Administration of High School Athletics,* 4th Ed., Prentice-Hall, Englewood Cliffs, N. J., 1962.

Gabrielson, M. Alexander, and Caswell, M. Miles, "Sports and Recreation facilities: For School and Community", Prentice-Hall, Englewood Cliffs, New Jersey, 1961.

Gatti, D., and Gatti, J., *The Teacher and the Law,* Parker Publishing Co., West Nyack, N. Y., 1972.

George, Jack F. and Lehmann, Harry A., *School Athletic Administration,* Harper and Row, New York, New York, 1966.

Golding, Lawrence A., and Bos, Ronald A., "Scientific Foundations of Physical Fitness", Burgess Publishing Co., Minneapolis, Minnesota, 1970.

Gorman, Patricia, "The Role of the Cheerleader", *The Ohio High School Athlete,* Columbus, Ohio, September, 1970.

Granger, Don E., "Motivation in Junior High Athletics", *The Coach,* Austin, Texas, August, 1970.

Griffin, J. H., and Jagg, William, "Stimulating Athletic Interest Through A Varsity Club", *Scholastic Coach,* May, 1960.

Hetrick, Tracy L., "An Old Game With A New Look", *The Ohio High School Athlete,* Columbus, Ohio, January, 1971.

Homola, Sam, "Muscle Training For Athletes", Parker Publishing Co., West Nyack, N. Y., 1971.

Horwitz, John J., "Team Practice and the Specialist", Charles C. Thomas Publishers, Springfield, Illinois, 1970.

How to Budget, Select, and Order Athletic Equipment, Athletic Goods Manufacturers Association, Chicago, Illinois, 1963.

Hunter, O. N., "The Safety Component in Education, "*Journal of Health, Physical Education, Recreation,* May, 1963.

Hyatt, Ronald W., "Evaluations in Intramurals", *Journal of Health, Physical Education, Recreation,* Washington, D. C., June, 1971.

Instructions for Care and Maintenance of Tartan Turf, 3 M Company, Recreation and Athletic Products, St. Paul, Minnesota, 1971.

James, Robert, "Evaluation of Coaches and Athletic Directors", *The Athletic Director,* National Council of Secondary School Athletic Directors, Washington, D. C., May, 1970.

Jaynson, D. Cyril, "A Guide for Games", *Sport-Shelf,* New Rochelle, New York, 1970.

Jenny, John, "Staff Responsibilities and Competencies", *Administration of High School Athletics–Report of A National Conference,* American Association for Health, Physical Education, and Recreation, Washington,. D. C., December, 1962.

Jernigan, Sara S., "The National Institute on Girls' Sports," *Journal of Health, Physical Education, Recreation,* June 1963.

Jokl, Ernst and Peter, "The Physiological Basis of Athletic Records," Charles C. Thomas Publisher, Sprinfield, Ill., 1968.

Kamenetz, Herman L., "The Wheelchair Book: Mobility for the Disabled," Charles C. Thomas Publisher, Springfield, Ill., 1969.

Keller, Ray J., "Making the Most of Your Old Facilities," *Journal of Health, Physical Education, Recreation,* Washington, D. C., June, 1971.

Kelley, Fred, "Isometric Drills for Strength and Power in Athletics," Parker Publishing Co., West Nyack, N. Y., 1971.

Kirk, Robert H., "Practical Aspects of Co-educational Intramurals," *The Physical Educator,* December, 1963.

Koenig, Fran, "Officiating in Girls' and Women's Sports," *Journal of Health, Physical Education, Recreation,* October 1963.

Kusserow, Jennie and Tebb, "Games as a Medium for World Understanding," *Journal Health, Physical Education, Recreation,* Washington, D. C., January, 1971.

LaGrand, Louis E., *Guide to Secondary School Discipline,* Parker Publishing Co., West Nyack, N. Y., 1969.

Larson, Knute, *School Discipline in an Age of Rebellion,* Parker Publishing Co., West Nyack, N. Y., 1972.

Larson, Robert L. and McMahn, R. O., "The Epiphysis and the Childhood Athlete," *Journal of American Medical Association,* 196:607-12, 1966.

Lessinger, Leon, "Every Kid a Winner: Accountability in Education," Simon and Schuster, Inc., New York, New York, 1970.

Maetozo, Matthew, G., "Required Specialized Preparation for Coaching," *Journal of Health, Physical Education, Recreation,* April, 1971.

Malumphy, Theresa, M., "Personality of Women Athletes in Intercollegiate Competition", *Research Quarterly,* October, 1968.

Meadows, Paul E., "Are We Really Coaching Fundamentals?" *Journal of Health, Physical Education, Recreation,* Washington, D. C., March, 1963.

Moore, J. W., "The Psychology of Athletic Coaching", Burgess Publishing Co. Minneapolis, Minnesota, 1970.

Morehouse, Chauncey A., "Sports Research Institute"—A Workable Model at Pennsylvania State University, *Journal of Health, Physical Education, Recreation,* Washington, D. C., January, 1971.

Morgan, William P., "Contemporary Readings in Sport Psychology", Charles C. Thomas, Publisher, Springfield, Illinois, 1970.

Morris, Don, *Kentucky High School Basketball,* Parker Publishing Co., West Nyack, N. Y., 1969.

Moser, Charles, *Policies and Procedures of Athletic Department,* Abilene, Texas Public Schools, Abilene, Texas, 1971.

Mudra, Darrell, "The Coach and the Learning Experience", *Journal of Health, Physical Education, Recreation,* Washington, D. C., May, 1970.

Mueller, Frederick O., and Robey, James M., "Factors Related to the Certification of High School Football Coaches", *Journal of Health, Physical Education, Recreation,* Washington, D. C., February, 1971.

Murray, Frank J., "Perpetual Inventory", *Scholastic Coach,* January 1962.

Neal, Patsy, "Coaching Techniques for Women," Addison-Wesley Publishing Co., Reading, Massachusetts, 1969.

Nolte, M. C., *Guide to School Law,* Parker Publishing Co., West Nyack, N. Y., 1969.

Ohio High School Athletic Association, *Constitution and Rules,* Columbus, Ohio, September, 1971.

Ohio High School Athletic Association, *Catastrophic Injury Policy,* Columbus, Ohio, 1971.

Ohio High School Athletic Association, *Student Insurance,* Doug Ruedlinger, Inc., Columbus, Ohio, 1971.

Olds, Glenn A., "In Defense of Sports", *Journal of Health, Physical Education, Recreation,* January, 1961.

Olson, Edward C., "Conditioning Fundamentals," Charles E. Merrill Publishing Co., Columbus, Ohio, 1968.

Olson, Edward C., "Individual Rights for the Coach," *Journal of Health, Physical Education, Recreation,* Washington, D. C., January, 1970.

Page, Anita, "Crossing Aesthetic Lines," *Journal of Health, Physical Education, Recreation,* Washington, D. C., September, 1970.

Perkins, James, *Athletic Department Policies and Procedures of Riverside-Brookfield Township High School,* Riverside, Illinois, 1970.

Planning Areas and Facilities for Health, Physical Education, and Recreation by Participants in National Facilities Conference, The Athletic Institute, Chicago, Illinois and American Association for Health, Physical Education, and Recreation, Washington, D. C., 1965.

Professional Preparation of the Administrator of Athletics, A Committee report–Division of Men's Athletics–American Association of Health, Physical Education, and Recreation, Washington D C., 1968.

Purdy, Robert L., *Policies and Procedures of Athletic Department* Berea City Schools, Berea, Ohio, 1971.

Rasch, Philip J., "Protein and the Athlete," *The Physical Educator,* December, 1960.

Rawlinson, Ken, "Modern Athletic Training," Parker Publishing Co., West Nyack, N. Y., 1971.

Richardson, Deane, E., "Preparation for a Career in Public School Athletic Administration," *Journal of Health, Physical Education, Recreation,* Washington, D. C., February, 1971.

Ruffer, William A., "Sumposium on Problems of the Black Athlete", *Journal of Health, Physical Education, Recreation,* Washington, D. C., April, 1971.

Ryan, Allan J., "Prevention of Sports Injury: A Problem Solving Approach", *Journal of Health, Physical Education, Recreation,* Washington, D. C., April, 1971.

Saback, Ralph J., "Perspiration and Inspiration," *The Ohio High School Athlete,* Columbus, Ohio, February, 1969.

Sage, George H., "Sport and American Society: Selected Readings," Addison-Wesley Publishing Co., Redding, Massachusetts, 1970.

Savastano, A. A., "Rhode Island Shows the Way; In-Service Training for the Prevention and Treatment of Athletic Injuries," *Journal of Health, Physical Education, Recreation,* Washington, D. C., April, 1970.

Schunk, Carol, "Interscholastics–Part of the Educative Process," *The Ohio High School Athlete,* Columbus, Ohio, February, 1969.

Schwab, Diana L., "Let's Teach Our Women Physical Education Majors How to Coach," *The Ohio High School Athlete,* Columbus, Ohio, May, 1970.

Secondary School Athletic Administration–A New Look–Report on Second National Conference on Secondary School Athletic Administration, *American Association, Health, Physical Education, and Recreation,* Washington, D. C., January, 1969.

Schaffer, Thomas E., M. C., "Principles of Growth and Development as Related to Girls Participating in Track and Field and Gymnastics," *Proceedings: First National Institute on Girls Sports,* Washington, D. C., AAHPER, 1964.

Shaffer, Thomas E., MD., "Are Little Leagues Good for Children?", *Pennsylvania Medical Journal,* 1956.

Simmons, Allan A., "Drug Use in Sports," *The Ohio High School Athlete,* Columbus, Ohio, February, 1971.

Sliger, Ira T., "An Extensive Sports Club Program," *Journal of Health, Physical Education, Recreation,* Washington, D. C., February, 1970.

Slovenko, Ralph, and Knight, James A., "Motivation in Play, Games, and Sports," Charles C. Thomas, Publishers, Springfield, Ill., 1967.

Smith, Gary, "Violence and Sport," *Journal of Health, Physical Education, Recreation,* Washington, D. C., March, 1971.

Smith, Rex B., *Policies and Procedures of Athletic Department,* Parma City schools, Parma, Ohio, 1971.

Sprague, Vernon S., "Cost Factors for Institutional Laundry Services," *Journal of Health, Physical Education, Recreation,* Washington, D. C., February, 1971.

Sports, Safety, American Association Health Physical Education, and Recreation Safety Education Division, 1971.

Standards for Junior High School Athletics, American Association of Health, Physical Education and Recreation, Washington, D. C., 1963.

Stewart, Ralph E., "Junior High School Athletics Comes of Age," *The Ohio High School Athlete,* Columbus, Ohio, February, 1970.

Stielstra, Jay, *Michigan-Style High School Football,* Parker Publishing Co., West Nyack, N. Y., 1969.

Stier, William F., Jr., "The Coaching Intern," *Journal of Health, Physical Education, Recreation,* Washington, D. C., January, 1970.

Suprina, Dick, "Student Statisticians," *Scholastic Coach,* September, 1962.

Talamo, Joe, and Roy Lupinacci, *Developing a Championship Football Program,* Parker Publishing Co., West Nyack, 1969.

Theibert, P. Richard, "The Facts About Synthetic Surfaces," *The Athletic Director,* Washington, D. C., December, 1970.

Thomas, Eugene S., "The Role of Athletics in Education," Administration of High School Athletics–*Report of a National Conference, American Association of Health, Physical Education, and Recreation,* Washington, D. C., December, 1963.

Thomas, G. Patience, "The Social Psychology of Sport: Groups Interaction,"

Thomas, Jack G., "Checklist for Athletic Directors," *The Physical Educator,* March, 1969.

Vander Zwagg, Harold, "Sports Concepts," *Journal of Health, Physical Education, Recreation,* Washington, D. C., March, 1970.

Vanek, Miroslav, and Cratty, Bryant J., "Psychology and the Superior Athlete," Macmillan Company, Riverside, New Jersey, 1970.

Veller, Don, "Avoiding Trip Headaches," *Scholastic Coach,* March, 1964.

Verderame, Sal., "Coach's Guide to Public Relations," Parker Publishing Co., West Nyack, N.Y., 1971.

Weiss, Raymond C., "Do Sports Produce Fitness," *Journal of Health, Physical Education, Recreation,* March 1961.

Whited, Clark V., "Sport Science," *Journal of Health, Physical Education, Recreation,* Washington, D. C., May, 1971.

Wilson, Kenneth "Tug", and Brondfield, Jerry, "The Big Ten," Parker Publishing Co., West Nyack, N. Y., 1971.

Yosinoff, Andrew, "The Problem of the Coach and the New Athlete," *The Ohio High School Athlete,* Columbus, Ohio, February, 1971.

Index

A

Accident plans, 192-197
Administration:
athletics, part of curriculum, 16-17
basic philosophy, 15-16
colleges, universities, 21
elementary schools, 20
interscholastic and intercollegiate athletic programs, 20-21
junior high schools, 20-21
professional personnel, 21
professional responsibility, 18-19
proper consideration of all sports, 16
rapport with coaches, 35-48
senior high schools, 21
superintendent and board of education, 17-18
Admission, right, 159-160
Affiliation, 122-125
Aims, 15
Amateur status, 119, 121
American Association for Health, Physical Education, and Recreation, 19, 46, 232, 233, 239
Annual athletic report, 33-34
Annual financial report, 72-74
Appendicitis, 196
Appreciation projects, 55
Approval, contests and travel, 185
Art department, 16
Artificial turf, 105-107
Assemblies, 24, 42, 173-174
Assistant coach, 32
Associations:
AAHPER, 232, 233
"Athletic Director," 18, 19, 46, 239
certification of secondary school coaches, 233-239
"Crowd Control in High School Athletics," 239
district, 240-241
Division of Men's Athletics of the American Association for Health, Physical Education, and Recreation, 19, 46, 233, 239
"Fellowship of Christian Athletes," 247
future trends in school athletics, 245-247
national, 167-168, 239
national code of ethics for high school coaches, 245
National Council of Secondary School Athletic Directors, 17, 18, 46, 239, 240
National Council of State High School Coaches, 233
policies governing attendance at clinics and meetings, 241-242
professional behavior of athletic directors, 242-244
professional preparation of athletic directors, 232-233
state, 167-168, 239-240
Athletic assocation, 69-72
Athletic Director, 18, 19, 46, 239
"Athletics in Education," 19
Athletic Inventory Record, 100
Attendance, clinics and meetings, 241-242
Audio, 148
Awards, 89, 174-177, 188, 207-211

B

Band, 150-151
Band concerts, 17
Banquets, 42, 53-54, 170-173
Bid buying procedures, 95-101 (*see also* Maintenance)
"Bill of Rights for the Athlete," 202
Board of education, 17-18, 33, 35-37, 65-66
Boosters club, 54-60, 61-65, 174
Brawling, 197
Breakfasts, victory, 215
Briggs, Paul, 16
Budget, 42 (*see also* Financing)
Buses:
chartering, 133-134
spectator, 134-136
transportation, 65

C

Car parkers, 139
Card, sports participation, 184
Cardiac disease, 196-197
Catastrophic insurance, 194-197
Certified teachers, 185-186, 233-239
Character, 187
Checks, 138
Cheerleader sponsor, 32
Cheerleaders, 147, 166-167
Cheerleading programs:
  award system, 207-210
  clinics, 203-204, 204-205
    local, in spring, 204-205
    state sponsored, 203-204
  eligibility, 210-211
  handbook, 211-214
    alternates, 213
    junior varsity squads, 213
    practice sessions, 212-213
    summer practices, 211-212
    supervision at games, 212
    transportation to away games, 213-214
    uniforms, 212
  promoting school spirit, 214-216
    mascot, 215
    other techniques, 215-216
    pep assemblies, 214
    pep clubs, 215
    signs, 214
    victory breakfasts, 215
  qualities judges look for, 205-107
  selection plan, 205
  special groups, 210
  summer camps, 204
Child growth and development, 21
Chorus, 17
Clinics, 43, 101-102, 241-242
Clubs, local service, 51-54
Coaches:
  assignment and supervision, 41-42
  capable classroom teachers, 17
  certified, 185-186, 233-239
  eligibility procedures, 115, 117
  employment, 40-41
  national code of ethics, 245
  professional preparation, 17
  rapport with administration, 35-48
  secondary school, 233-239
Coaching staff, 165-166
Co-educational activities, 185
Colleges, 21
Collins, H. Roger, 199
Communication channels:
  annual athletic report, 33-34
  handbook, 23-33 (*see also* Handbook)
  manuals, 33
  monthly reports to board of education, 33
Communication system, 17
Community involvement, 163-165
Competition, 186
Complimentary ticket holder, 162
Concessions, 139
Conduct, 187
Conferences:
  affiliation, 122-125
  individual with staff members, 42
Construction, facilities, 101-104
Content areas, 80
Contest rules, 169
Conventions, 43
Cooperation, 91-92
Crowd control:
  after event, 158-159
  appreciate skill in performance, 169
  athletic directors, 165
  cheerleaders, 166-167
  coaching staff, 165-166
  community involvement, 163-165
  during event, 155-157
  duty owed to invitees and licensees, 160-161
  fundamentals of sportsmanship, 168-169
  law and spectator, 159-163
  legal status of spectator, 159-160
  officials, 167
  planned procedure, 153-165
  players, 166
  prior to event, 153-155
  problems, 16
  respect for officials, 169
  respect for opponent, 168-169
  right to admission, 159-160
  rules of contest, 169
  self-control, 169
  state and national associations, 167-168
  status of complimentary ticket holder, 162
  status of gate crasher, 162-163
  status of ticket buyer, 160-162
  "supportive" people, 165
"Crowd Control in High School Athletics," 239
Curriculum, 16-17
Custodial responsibilities, 146-147

D

Day game procedures, 137-151 (*see also* game procedures)
Death, 196
Debate, 17
Dental expense, 196
Detached retina, 197
Development, child, 21
Diabetes, 197
Director, 17, 18, 19, 27-28, 38-40, 113-115
Dirt removal, 105-106
Dismemberment, 196
District, associations, 240-241
Division of Men's Athletics, 19, 46, 233, 239
Doctors, 25, 66, 138, 144-146, 149
Dressing rooms, 102-103
Drying rooms, 103

E

Electives, 80
Elementary schools, 20
Eligibility, 25, 42, 88-89, 187, 210-211
Eligibility procedures:
- basic responsibility, 108-109
- coahces' cooperation, 115, 117
- communication with teachers, 113
- each building, 109, 111, 113
- maintaining amateur status, 119, 121
- participation forms, 117, 119
- role of athletic director, 113-115
- status of ineligible player, 117

Equipment, 83, 93-107 (*see also* Maintenance)
Ethics, national code, 245
Evaluation, program, 43-48
Evaluative instruments, 86
Examinations, physical, 197-199
Exercise, effects, 21
Exhibits, 17
Eyes, loss, 196

F

Facilities, 17, 83, 93-107 (*see also* Maintenance)
Faculty representatives, 186
Fall, 90
Feet, loss, 196
"Fellowship of Christian Athletes," 247
Field, 148, 186
Fighting, 197
Film, football, 54-55
Financing:
- annual financial report, 72-74
- board of education, 65-66
- Boosters Club, 61-65
- bus transportation, 65
- disbursement of funds, 62
- expenses, 64-65
- final budget, 70
- girls' interscholastic athletics, 185
- income, 63-64
- medical doctors, 66
- money raising projects, 66, 67-68
- monthlv reports, 75
- more boys on existing teams, 66
- new senior or junior high schools, 66
- new sports added, 66
- overscheduling reams, 66
- physical education department budget, 69
- police protection bills, 66
- public tax monies, 65
- purchase order, 74-75
- raffles, 66
- responsibility of athletic association, 69-72
- safety items, 65-66
- service clubs, 66-67

First aid, 21
Football film, 54-55
Forms, athletic participation, 187
Friday activities, 85-86
Funds (*see* Financing)
Future, trends, 245-247

G

Game procedures:
- adult and student car parkers, 139
- audio and video, 148
- band, 150-151
- basic check list, 137-139, 148-149
- checks-workers and officials, 138
- cheerleaders, 147
- concessions, 139
- crowd control, 152-169 (*see also* Crowd control)
- custodial responsibilities, 146-147
- doctor and trainer, 138, 144-146, 149
- field, 148
- gate help, 139, 140
- general adm. tickets, 138
- lights, 149
- money, 138
- officials, 139, 142-144, 149
- phones, 139
- police, 139, 142

Game procedures (*cont.*)
press box, 138
programs and sellers, 138, 141-142, 149
punches, tape, hammer, 138
res. sec. tickets, 138
season tickets, 138
signs, 138
stadium, 148
stretcher, 138
supply items, 149
tacks, pencils, 138
ticketboard, 139
trunk for games away, football, 146
ushers, 139, 140-141
Gate help, 139, 140
Girls Athletic Association, 90-91
Girls' interscholastic athletics:
administration, 182-183
agreement conditions, 181-182
general program, 177-180
proposed organizational guidelines, 180-181
rules and regulations, 183-189
approval of contests and travel, 185
approved rules, 183
athletic awards, 188
athletic participation forms required, 187
certificated teachers, 185-186
character or conduct, 187
co-educational activities, 185
competition, 187
eligibility list, 187
faculty representative, 186
finances, 185
limit of participation, 188
officials, 186
recognized sports, 186
regulations, 189
rule coverage, 183-184
scholarship, 187
violation of rules, 189
Grade level, 183
Group action, 18
Growth, child, 21
Guest nights, 52-53
Gymnasium:
details, 102
dressing rooms, 102-103
boys, 102
girls, 103
equipment drying rooms, 103
laundry room, 104
lobby, 102
offices. 103
Gymnasium (*cont.*)
supply room, 103
swimming pool, 103-104
training room, 103
Gymnastics, 186

H

Hammer, 138
Handbook:
area assignments, 23-26
assemblies, 24
assistant coach, 32
cheerleader sponsor, 32
cheerleading, 211-214
director of athletics, 27-28
doctors and medical attention, 25
duties and responsibilities of key athletic personnel, 26-32
eligibility, 25
format, 26
head coach, 29-32
policies and procedures, 22-23
secondary school principals, 27
senior high school faculty manager of athletics, 29
table of contents, 23-24
use, 33
Hands, loss, 196
Head coach, 29-32
Hernia, 196
Hesche, Neal, 80
High schools, 20-21
Hospital expense, 196

I

Implementation, new procedures, 42-43
"In-breeding," 40
Income (*see* Financing)
Independent teams, 184
Infections, secondary, 197
Injury, 195, 197
Injury report, 198
Instructions to bidders, 98-99
Insurance and medical assistance, 190-202
Intercollegiate athletic programs, 20-21
Interscholastic athletic programs, 20-21, 177-189 (*see also,* Girls' interscholastic athletics)
Intramural activities, 17, 43
Intramural program:
assignment of personnel, 92
awards, 89
coooperation, 91-92
duties of directors, 87-88

Intramural program (*cont.*)
- eligibility standards, 88-89
- general procedures, 89
- Girls Athletic Association, 90-91
- insurance form questionnaire, 88
- sports activities, 89-90

J

James, Bob, 46
Joint projects, 16-17
Junior high school athletics:
- administrative responsibility, 225
- association with other schools, 229-230
- conditioning period, 227
- eligibility, 224-225
- equipment, 227
- facilities, 227
- grade limitation, 224
- interscholastic, 218-221
- meets and tournaments, 225-226
- night contests, 226
- officials, 226
- operative purposes, 225
- participating limitations, 226
- participation on high school team, 225
- physical examination, 226-227
- point of view, 222-223
- points of agreement, 218
- policies and principles governing administration, 223-224
- preliminaries or exhibitions, 225
- program offered, 227-228
- rules and regulations, 224-227
- safety measures, 226-227
- semester attendance rule, 225
- standards, 217-218
- state athletic association, 221-227

K

Kiwanis Club, 51-52

L

Laundry room, 104
Law, 159-163
League, affiliation, 122-125
Legislation, 16
Life, loss, 196
Lights, 149
Litter removal, 105
Lobby, gymnasium, 102
Local service clubs, 51-54
Lowry, Richard, 80

M

Maintenance:
- artificial turf, 105-107
  - dirt removal, 105-106
  - litter removal, 105
  - removal of water, 106
  - shampooing, 105
  - snow removal, 106
  - stain removal, 106, 107
- basic principles, 93-94
- bid buying procedures, 95-101
  - athletic inventory record, 100
  - cleaning and reconditioning, 95, 101
  - form of proposal, 99
  - instructions to bidders, 98-99
  - notice to bidders, 98
  - requesting items, 95
  - specifications and bid sheets, 97
- facilities construction, 101-104
  - clinic, 101-102
  - gymnasium, 102-103 (*see also* Gymnasium)
- program, 104-105
- specific guidelines, 94-95

Malignancy, 197
Manuals, use, 33
Mascot, 215
Meals, 134
Medical assistance, insurance and, 190-202
Medical attention, 25, 66
Medicine, sports, 200-202
Meetings, staff, 42
"Middle man" (*see* Director)
Money (*see* Financing)
Monies, public tax, 16
Monthly financial report, 75
Monthly reports to board of education, 33
Moser, Charles, 58-59

N

National associations, 239
National Council of Secondary School Athletic Directors, 17, 18, 46, 239, 240
National Council of State High School Coaches, 233
National Education Association, 19
Notice to bidders, 98

O

Objectives, 15
Observation form, 44

Offices, gymnasium, 103
Officials:
- assignment, 127-132
- checks, 138
- communication, 133
- contract forms, 131, 132
- criticizing, 127
- crowd control, 167
- delay in employing, 131
- emergency situations, 130
- final decision on hiring, 131
- game procedures, 139, 142-144, 149
- games with seasonal men, 130
- girls' interscholastic athletics, 186
- good standing, 127
- head coaches consulted, 131
- inexperienced, 130
- interpretations of rules, 130
- keep players and coaches informed, 130
- pattern of employing, 130
- poor treatment, 132
- position when making calls, 130
- prompt, reliable, cooperative, 130
- reports, 133
- respect for, 169
- safety conscious, 130
- same for number of games, 131
- special instructions, 133
- specific assignments, 130, 131
- treatment and cooperation, 132-133
- type of man employed, 130
- uniforms, 130
- unusual circumstances or events, 133
- varsity football, 131
- well qualified in sport, 127
- work hard, 130
- OHSAA, 192-197
- Opponent, respect, 168-169

Organization, administration, 15-21 (*see also* Administration)
Osgood-Schlatter's Disease, 197
Osteomyelitis, 197
Overscheduling teams, 66

P

Parents, honoring, 55-57
Parkers, car, 139
Participation:
- boys and girls, 17
- limit, 188

Participation forms, eligibility procedures, 117, 119
Penalties, 189
Pencils, 138
Pep assemblies, 214
Pep clubs, 215
Perkins, James, 38
Personnel, assignment, 92
Personnel director, 37-38
Personnel policies:
- assistant coach, 32
- cheerleader sponsor, 32
- director of athletics, 27-28
- head coach, 29-32
- secondary school principals, 27
- senior high school faculty manager of athletics, 29

Personnel, professional, 21
Philosophy, basic, 15-16, 17, 19
Phones, 139
Physical education department, budget, 69
Physical education program:
- cooperation, 91-92
- development, 77-86
- implementation, 83-86
  - equipment and supplies, 83
  - evaluative instruments, 86
  - Friday activities, 85-86
  - plan, 84-86
  - regulatory factors, 83
  - space and facilities, 83
  - subject areas offered for each six-week period, 84-85
  - teacher-student assignments, 83
  - time allotment, 83
- needs of high school students, 78-80
  - physiological nature of student, 79
  - physiological principles, 78
  - psychological nature of student, 79-80
  - psychological principles, 78
  - sociological principles, 78-79
- personnel, assignment, 92
- terminology, 80-83
  - content areas, 80
  - electives, 80
  - prerequisite, 82
  - requirements, 80-81
  - subject areas, 80
  - time blocks, 82-83
  - unit requirement, 81-82

Physical examinations, 197-199
Physician, 25, 66, 138, 144-146, 149
Physiological principles, 78, 79
Plays, one act, 17
Police, 139, 142, 152-169 (*see also* Crowd control)
Police protection bills, 66
Policies and procedures:
- anjual athletic report, 33-34

Policies and procedures (*cont.*)
committee involved in developing, 22-23
handbook, 23-33 (*see also* Handbook)
manuals, use, 33
monthly reports to board of education, 33
Pool, swimming, 103-104
Prerequisite, 82
Press, 49-50, 138
Principals:
cooperation with personnel director, 37-38
secondary school, 27
Principles, administration, 15-21 (*see also* Administration)
Procedures, new 42-43 (*see also* Policies and procedures)
Professional personnel, 21
Professional responsibility, 18-19
Programs, sellers, 138, 141-142, 149
Projects, joint, 16-17
Protests, 189
Psychological principles, 78, 79
Public relations:
boosters club, 54-57
appreciation projects, 55
cooperation on projects, 54
football film, 54-55
honoring parents, 55-57
general procedures, 58-60
local service clubs, 51-54
Berea Kiwanis Club, 51-52
co-sponsor banquets, 53-54
guest nights, 52-53
guidelines, 51
press, radio, television, 49
prompt communication, 49-50
special consideration, 50
student reporters, 50
Public tax monies, 16, 65
Punches, 138
Purchase order, 74-75
Purdy, Robert, 65

R

Radio, 49-50
Raffles, 66
Regulations:
girls' interscholastic athletics, 183-189 (*see also* Girls' interscholastic athletics)
junior high school athletics, 224-227
Reporters, student, 50
Reports:
annual athletic, 33-34
annual financial, 72-74
monthly financial, 75
monthly, to board of education, 33
Requirements, 80-81
Reserved section, 50
Responsibility, professional, 18-19
Retina, detached, 197
Rules:
girls interscholastic athletics 183-189 (*see also* Girls' interscholastic athletics)
junior high school athletics, 224-227

S

Safety items, 65-66
Scheduling:
basic rules, 126-127
create good rivalry, 126
crowd control, 127
football, 126
good sportsmanship, 127
home and away games, 126
junior varsity and junior high school games, 126
regulate, 126
specific terms in contracts, 127, 128, 129
strength of competition, 127
teams with good following, 126
treatment by home school, 127
type of competition, 126
Scholarship, 187
Scrimmage, 184
Secondary school principals, 27
Senior high school faculty manager of athletics, 29
Senior high schools, 21
Service clubs, 51-54, 66-67, 174
Shaffer, Thomas E., 200, 202
Shampooing, artificial turf, 105-106
Sight, loss, 196
Signs, 138, 214
Smith, Rex B., 44, 65
Snow removal, 106
Sociological principles, 78
Space, 83
Specifications and bid sheets, 97
Sponsorship, 183-184
Sports activities, 89-90
Sports medicine, 200-202
Sportsmanship, 168-169
Spring, 90
Stadium, 148

Staff meetings, 42
Stain removal, 106, 107
State associations, 239-240
Status:
  amateur, 119, 121
  ineligible player, 117
Stretcher, 138
Student reporters, 50
Subject areas, 80, 84-85
Superintendent of schools, 17-18, 35-37
Supplies, 83
Supply items, 149
Supply room, gymnasium, 103
"Supportive" people, 165
Swimming, 186
Swimming pool, 103-104

T

Tacks, 138
Tape, 138
Tax monies, public, 16, 65
Teacher-student assignments, 83
Television, 49-50
Thinnes, Nelson, 65
Ticketboard, 139
Tickets, 138
Time blocks, 82-83
Track, 186
Training room, gymnasium, 103
Transportation, bus, 65 (*see also* Buses)
Travel, approval, 185
Trunk, football, 146
Tryouts, cheerleaders, 205-207
Turf, 105-107

U

Unit requirements, 81-82
Universities, 21
Ushers, 139, 140-141

V

Victory breakfasts, 215
Video, 148

W

Water, removal, 106
Winter, 90
Workshops, 43